# ENGLISH SNUFF-BOXES

# ENGLISH

# SNUFF-BOXES

—

G. Bernard Hughes

MacGibbon & Kee   London

Granada Publishing Limited
First published in Great Britain 1971 by MacGibbon & Kee Ltd
3 Upper James Street London WIR 4BP

ISBN 0 261 63227 2
Printed in Great Britain by Ebenezer Baylis & Son Ltd
The Trinity Press, Worcester, and London

For My Good Friend
GWENOCH TALBOT

# CONTENTS

# ILLUSTRATIONS

# CHAPTER I

# Introduction

ELEGANT Englishmen of Tudor and Stuart days seldom stirred from home without pomander or perfumed pouncet box. From these they could inhale aromatic perfumes to counteract the community's unsavoury odours. Until early in the reign of James I (1603–25) men carried them attached to black cord or in the pocket. Fashion evolved a prescribed procedure for handling these jewels and this eventually became virtually a ceremonial ritual. Perfume was superseded in the pouncet box from the 1590s by coarsely ground tobacco leaves.

This powder, snuffed up the nostrils, had quickly established itself as a pungent protection against various maladies. The word *snuff* is an inflexion of the old northern verb *sniff* – a term that described strong inhalation through the nostrils or expressing angry impatience long before the introduction of powdered tobacco leaves.

The story that Sir Walter Raleigh (1552–1618) introduced tobacco into England has no basis in fact. In 1584, the very year in which Ralegh founded the colony of Virginia, Queen Elizabeth issued a decree, still preserved in the Public Record Office, condemning the use and abuse of tobacco. The smoking of tobacco appears to have been customary in England twenty years earlier, for in 1563 the Statute of Labourers laid down that no man or woman should be employed in making clay tobacco pipes without serving a five-year apprenticeship in the craft. The inference may be drawn that tobacco-smoking in England dates from late in the reign of Henry VIII. When Ralegh, at the age of eighteen, was appointed a gentleman volunteer in the army, tobacco was actually being grown in England. Its culture was recorded by Matthias de l'Obel and

Petrus Pena in their book published in London during 1570:
l'Obel later became chief botanist to James I.

By the end of the 16th century the powdered snuff was
carried in a small box with a tightly fitting hinged lid. Such
boxes were elegant trifles for the well-to-do and were successors
of the gold pouncet box. More modestly they were made in
pewter, horn and latten. Harrison's *Chronicle* in 1580 described
snuff-taking as 'the taking-in of the finely pulverised Indian
herbe called Tabaco by an instrument formed like a little
ladell.' Dekker in his *Gulls Horne-booke*, 1609, confirmed the use
of the ladle or snuff-spoon: 'the gallant must draw out his
tobacco-box, the ladle for the cold snuff into the nostril. . . . '

In his *Counterblaste to tobacco*, 1604, James I complained that
peers and rich merchants were spending several hundred pounds
a year on tobacco and snuff. In an effort to discourage this
luxury the king placed tobacco under a royal monopoly and
increased excise duty from twopence to 6s 10d per lb, its shop
price then being about 3s 4d per oz – almost as much as a labour-
er's weekly wage. Even so, ten years later nearly 7,000 London
shops, vintners and alehouses were retailing tobacco. This
naturally encouraged the production of tax-free native-grown
tobacco and in 1615 a pamphlet was published: 'An Advise how
to plant Tobacco in England: and how to bring it to colour and
perfection, to whom it may be profitable and to whom harmful.'

In the same year Joshua Sylvester, court poet to James I, was
denouncing snuff as 'hell-dust, England's shame, a madness, a
frenzy, that by the devil's agency has been brought from the
savages to England'. Tobacco was eventually cultivated in
about forty English and Scottish counties. Charles II, however,
condemned native tobacco-growing as a penal offence in the
1660s.

At this time snuff became known colloquially as 'snush', a
term continued into the Georgian period. An advertisement in
the *London Gazette* in 1682 announced the loss of 'a Round Gold
Snush-Box'. Ned Ward in *The London Spy* a few years later,
invariably used the term snush when commenting upon the use of

snuff-boxes in London coffee-houses. Of one eminent but un-named establishment he wrote: 'We squeezed thro' the Flutter-ing Assembly of Snuffing Peripateticks . . . the Clashing of their Snush-Box Lids, in opening and shutting made more noise than their Tongues: and sounded as Terrible in my Ears as the Melancholy Ticks of so many Death Watches.' Later he noticed the demand for 'perfumed snushes'.

So far snuff had always been rasped by the purchaser of the carotte of tobacco leaves or else bought ready-powdered from foreign hawkers. Charles Lillie, a perfumer and tobacconist of the Strand, London, in 1702 recorded the capture of about fifty tons of milled snuff from Spanish ships at anchor in Vigo Bay and at Port St Mary. Lillie wrote: 'This sort of bale snuff had never been seen or known in England before, except through the Spanish Jews who in the present case, bought up almost the whole quantity at a considerable advantage. From the quantity of snuff thus distributed throughout the kingdom, novelty being quickly embraced by us in England, arose the custom and fashion of snuff-taking.' Lillie described snuff-taking as being 'chiefly a luxurious habit among foreigners residing here, and the English gentry who have travelled abroad. Amongst these the mode of taking the snuff is with pipes of the size of quills out of small spring boxes. These pipes let out a very small quantity of snuff upon the back of the hand, and this is snuffed up the Nostrils with the intention of producing sneezing, which I need not say forms now no part of the design or rather fashion of snuff-taking.'

During the next decade snuffing became an important social accomplishment. Schools were established for teaching the now fashionable art of snuff-taking. An advertisement inserted by Charles Lillie in No. 138 of *The Spectator*, 1711, outlines the curriculum of his school: 'The exercise of the snuff-box accord-ing to the most fashionable airs and motions, in opposition to the exercise of the fan, will be taught with the best plain or per-fumed snuff, at Lillie's, perfumer in the Strand, and attendance given for the benefit of young merchants about the Exchange, for two hours every day at noon, at a toy shop near Garraway's Coffee-house. There will be taught the ceremony of the snuff-box, rules for offering snuff to a stranger, a friend, or a mistress, with an explanation of the careless, the scornful, the politic and the surly pinch, and the gestures proper to each of them.'

Horace Walpole's collection of snuff-boxes in the mid-century included an oval and 'a square-shaped snuff-box of lapis lazuli mounted in gold; a circular gold snuff-box, engine-turned, with the image in wax of Madame la Marquise du Deffand's dog Tonton' which she bequeathed to Walpole.

The approved method of taking snuff evolved at this time continued until its decline in the 1860s. The snuff-box was carried in the left hand waistcoat pocket from which it was withdrawn with the right hand and passed to the left hand. The user gave the lid three smart taps near the hinge, opened the box and inspected the contents. A pinch of snuff was then taken and held for a second or two between thumb and first finger of the right hand while the box was closed and put away, so that the pinch of powder could be placed on the back of the left hand or on the thumb-nail and inhaled by both nostrils simultaneously without any grimace. Less elegantly but more commonly, however, the snuff was carried directly to the nose and snuffed with each nostril in turn. By this method the final gesture could be to close the box with a flourish. Sneezing formed no part of fashionable snuff-taking. The preliminary tapping of the snuff-box was to attract the powder away from the opening of the essentially tight-fitting lid and so avoid an undignified cloud of dust. The complete ritual was outlined in an anonymous pamphlet of 1750.

The fashionable Georgian snuff-taker selected his snuff from a wide range of ready-made snuff rather than rasping his own: sweet, strong or salt; fine, medium or coarse; dry, semi-moist or moist; and scented with lemon, jasmine, orange flowers, rose, verbena, bergamot or cloves. Many snuffers enriched the character of their snuff by adding such ingredients as mustard, ginger, ambergris or green tea. More commonly inexpensive snuff was perfumed by carrying a fragrant tonka bean in the snuff-box. Sold as 'snuff-beans' these were black almond-shaped seeds from the *dipterix odurata* tree of Guiana.

The most popular of the finer snuffs was macouba, dispensed by snuffmen who ground and sifted together 40 parts of French or St Omer tobacco leaves with 20 parts of powdered fermented Virginian stalks. To this was added 2½ parts of finely powdered rose petals. The whole was then moistened with salt and water and thoroughly incorporated. After being worked up with salts of tartar it was packed in lead foil to preserve its delicate aroma.

A bill from Fribourg & Treyer, who have operated at No. 34 Haymarket since 1720, to Lord Pelham, dated 21 August 1787, states that they 'Make and Sell all Sorts of French Rappees, Spanish, Portuguese, Scotch and High Dry'd Irish Snuffs'. One of the most fashionable snuffs sold here throughout the reign of George III (1760–1820) was Spanish bran at three guineas a pound. This snuff was accompanied by a two shilling phial of vinagrillo, an aromatic rose-scented vinegar imported from Spain. Small quantities were used to moisten the Spanish bran.

Fastidious snuff-takers laid down snuff as they laid down cellars of wine, many reserving a small room specially for storing snuffs and preparing them for daily use. The Earl of Harrington, formerly Lord Petersham and a celebrated snuff connoisseur, left snuff in his cabinets to the value of more than £3,000 when he died in 1829. He prided himself that he possessed a jewelled snuff-box for every day of the year. To a friend who expressed admiration for his snuff-box of light blue Sèvres porcelain, he commented, 'Yes, it's a nice box for summer, but would not do for winter use'. The connoisseur considered that the quality used during the morning was unsuitable for evening enjoyment: his cabinets contained morning and evening snuffs and for each an appropriate spoon.

When snuff-taking was at its height the *Ladies Journal* calculated in 1788 that the habitual snuff-taker took a pinch every ten minutes and this, with the ceremony of blowing and wiping the nose, occupied one and a half minutes. The editor declared that

2

in a snuff-taking life of forty years, two years would be dedicated to 'tickling the nose' and two more years to blowing it. The same magazine in 1823 vigorously attacked the practice of snuffing by ladies, stating that 'it bestows a cadaverous hue upon the complexion; destroys the sense of smell, stops up the nose, leaves a dirty patch on the upper lip, causes snuffing and grunting. In the case of men, ladies can never return a snuff-taker's kiss'.

Professor Ure in the 1830s discussed the prevalence of adulterated snuff despite legislation making this unlawful. He declared that snuff he had analysed contained a large proportion of starch and cereals, peameal, bran, sawdust, malt, rootlets, fustic, even ground glass and the deadly oxide of lead. Also sold ready prepared to snuff-makers were milled refuse leaves such as those of senna and rhubarb, coloured with burnt sienna and yellow ochre and made pungent with ammonia.

More than a century after rasped tobacco had first become established as a pungent perfume the snuff-box became a flamboyant accessory among the fashionable. It was Beau Nash who dazzled the nobility and rich gentry with his elegant handling of jewelled snuff-boxes after he was made Master of Ceremonies at Bath in 1704.

Oliver Goldsmith in his *Life of Richard Nash* recorded that in 1738 the Prince of Wales, in appreciation of the delights of Bath, presented Nash with a large gold enamelled snuff-box. 'Upon this some of the nobility thought it would be proper to give snuff-boxes, too: they were quickly imitated by the middling gentry and soon it became the fashion to give Nash snuff-boxes.' Many ladies at Bath were compulsive snuff-takers. Before stepping into the water the visitor was presented with a small floating dish in which she placed her snuff-box and handkerchief for use whilst traversing the bath.

Snuff-boxes were made in a wide range of materials from costly chased gold to inexpensive pewter and horn. Prior in his *Cupid and Ganymede*, 1709, described a snuff-box 'set with Bleeding Hearts and Rubies, all pierc'd with diamond darts'. Snuff-box design was glamorised by artist-jewellers creating an unceasing flow of new patterns in almost every branch of industrial art. This was ridiculed in a notice published in *The Tatler*, 7 March, 1710, regarding gold snuff-boxes displayed in the shops at that time, stating that 'a new edition will be put out on Saturday next, which will be the only one in fashion until after Easter. The gentleman that gave fifty pounds for the box set with diamonds may show it till Sunday, provided he goes to church, but not after that time, there being one to be published on Monday which will cost four-score guineas. They were made by the celebrated gold chaser, Charles Mather,' who was known as 'Bubble Boy'.

When the elaborate social ritual of the snuff-box had become acceptable in the drawing room, goldsmiths, chasers and jewellers created boxes resplendent with precious stones and gems. Gold and silver were set with flashing jewels as gifts for ladies. Many of these elegant small boxes, however, were intended as bonbonnières, to contain breath-sweetening comfits and it is difficult to distinguish these from snuff-boxes. By the mid-18th century similar boxes might be used, too, to contain sponges soaked in aromatic vinegar. Sir Ambrose Heal's collection of trade cards contains illustrations of several such 'spunge boxes'.

*The London Tradesman* by R. Campbell, 1747, describes the work of the 'snuff-Man who buys Tobacco from the Tobacconist, and makes it into several Sorts of Snuff, by cutting it small with an Engine, drying it before the Fire, and grinding it in a Mill. He seldom takes an Apprentice, but employs Labourers, who work at so much a Pound. This Trade is abundantly profitable, but now much over-stocked'. Campbell also adds that 'the Tobacconist's skill consists in recognizing the Properties of Tobacco, and his profit arises from the Difference between buying and selling. If they take any apprentices they are taught to cut, with an engine for the purpose, are employed in stripping the Leaf off the Stems and in spinning the Pig-Tail: it requires neither much Strength nor Ingenuity. The Trade is reputable and profitable and requires a large stock to set up with.' Labourers were paid twelve shillings a week for operating the 'engine' and preparing the tobacco for use.

Snuff now began to be ground in factory mills operated by horses walking round in never-ceasing circles. I observed this mode of power in use as late as the 1930s. Several mills might be seen at work in a single factory, each grinding about 30 lb of snuff each day. The tobacco stalks and leaves were first chopped by hand, piled into heaps, moistened and covered with cloths in a warm room where they were left to ferment for several weeks. After high fermentation this mass was reduced to dust in large wood-lined iron mortars, ground by heavy slowly moving pestles. This tobacco dust formed the basis for many types of snuff.

In 1747 too, *A General Description of All Trades* devoted a paragraph to Georgian snuff-box makers. 'The introduction of snuffing gave rise to and made these Artists become necessary, who have not been wanting from time to time to invent a great Variety of Fashions, but also to bring them to surprising degrees of beautiful workmanship, in all manner of Metals, Stones, Shells, who are continually striving to improve and vary them, in order to strike the Taste of the Curious.

'Their Work is easy, but very ingenious, the masters of which are not very numerous, though they take Apprentices. Their working hours are usually from six to nine, in which time a good hand will earn 3s or 4s, but in common not above 2s. A man may set up for himself with about £20.'

The trade card of Anne Vict and Thomas Mitchell, Cornhill, advertised in 1742 that they made 'Snuff-boxes of Gold, Silver, Mother of Pearl, Tortoiseshell, Agat, Amber, Ivory, &c.'. No classification of shapes by period is possible. To speak of the rounds of Queen Anne, the ovals of George I or the rectangles of George II is wrong for these were the prevailing shapes throughout the entire period and nearly every geometrical form is represented.

Snuff-boxes were necessarily carried close to the body as the chill must be taken from snuff to bring out its bouquet. Special snuff-box pockets were incorporated in clothing. Dean Swift in 1712 recorded that when he bought a new gold snuff-box 'the Duchess of Hamilton made me Pockets like a woman's, with a Belt and Buckle, for you know that I wear no wastcoat in Summer: and there are severall divisions, and one on purpose for my box'. Seven years later Tom D'Urfy wrote that 'a wench gave snuff to me out of her Placket pocket' – a small pocket inserted in the skirt. More usually the lady carried her snuff-box in a large pocket tied round the waist under the skirt. Not until the late 1790s did slender fashions require an alternative to this bulky pocket in the shape of the small handbag, known as an 'indispensible'. In 1799 *The Times* noted the new fashion for carrying a small bag to contain handkerchief, snuff-box and other necessities.

George IV was, like his mother Queen Charlotte, a copious snuffer: twelve varieties of fresh snuff were placed upon his wine table each day. During his Regency and reign he collected several hundred magnificent gold and jewelled snuff-boxes, most of which Queen Victoria had converted into personal jewellery. His Civil List expenditure on snuff-boxes was £7,000 a year and complaints were made by Parliament that he presented snuff-boxes to the value of about £15,000 to ministers on the signing of any treaty.

In the reign of William IV (1830–37) snuffing ceased to be a highly fashionable accomplishment associated with the nobility. Costly snuff-boxes were becoming personal accessories of the newly industrial rich. *Hints on Etiquette*, 1835, referred to snuff-taking as 'an idle, dirty habit, practised by stupid people in the unavailing endeavour to clear their stolid intellect and as it is not a custom particularly offensive to their neighbours, it may be left to each individual taste as to whether it be continued or not. An *Elégant* cannot take much snuff without decidedly losing caste.'

Very few snuff-boxes were seen at the Great Exhibition, 1851. Those catalogued were in silver, elaborately ornamented in high relief, then once more hand-worked: there was a renewed vogue for classic scenes such as Daphne teaching Chloe to play the flute. For everyday use the most common size was little more than half-an-inch thick and a couple of inches long. Wooden tobacco pipes came into extensive use during the 1850s bringing about a lessening demand for the fashionable snuffs.

### PRICES

The economist Dr Franz Pick affirmed in 1970 that antique snuff-boxes sold in 1969 showed a 75 per cent increase over the values of the previous year. The value of diamonds during the same period rose by only 20 per cent. The magnitude of this appreciation makes it impossible to value closely snuff-boxes that fall within the collector's orbit.

Astronomical prices were reached in 1969. A gold snuff-box made in 1726, its lid set with a tortoiseshell panel enriched with a monogram in diamonds, sold for £23,000. In May of that year Christies sold an ornate gold snuff-box made in 1744 for 16,000 guineas. A millionaire might pay as much as £4,000 for an early Georgian snuff-box of jewelled gold in which to carry his pep pills, whereas his secretary would perforce be satisfied with a mid-19th century box of tortoiseshell set in a silver plated nickel mount costing a pound or so.

Antique snuff-boxes in gold are comparatively rare and always very costly. A George I (1714–27) example, three inches wide, its cover chased with a Mercury and Argus scene enclosed in borders chased with scrolling foliage, was sold in 1970 for 820 guineas. A gold box, chased and dated 1736, bought a few years ago for £2 made 500 guineas in the sale rooms during 1968. Early 19th-century snuff-boxes are sometimes equally valuable. An engine-turned example made by A. J. Strachan, London, in 1803 sold for 440 guineas in 1970 and another by the same maker hallmarked 1827, for 660 guineas.

Here are a few prices obtained by Christies early in 1970 for factory-made silver snuff-boxes of collectors' quality:

Peter & Anne Bateman, London, 1791. Gilt, oval, cover chased with classical figures in relief within a *rocaille* cartouche. Width three inches. 170 guineas.

Samuel Pemberton, Birmingham, 1805. Decorated with scrolls and foliage on an engraved ground within a Greek key pattern border. 25 guineas. Snuff-boxes of this popular type are not rare.

Matthew Linwood, Birmingham, 1808. Plain with moulded sides and the cover set with a jasper plaque. Width 2½ in. 40 guineas.

Thropp & Taylor, Birmingham, 1812. Gilt with incurved sides and panels chased with diapered oak foliage. Width 2¾ in. 150 guineas.

A series of press-embossed views dating from the William IV period fell within the £30–£50 range. The embossment on those by Thomas Spice was so exaggerated that parts of the view projected as much as a quarter of an inch above the lid. Values of these reached as much as 100 guineas.

The condition of the hall-marks on silver snuff-boxes affects their collectors' interest. Examples struck with a set of hallmarks difficult to decipher lose up to 50 per cent of their market value.

Gold mounted rock crystal is now rare. A Mayfair jeweller in 1970 paid 820 guineas for a barrel-shaped example of the late 18th century. Bloodstone snuff-boxes, fashionable throughout the Georgian period, are always costly. A gold-mounted snuff-box set top and bottom with a bloodstone and hallmarked 1740 sold for 350 guineas; a London-made example with its surface engine-turned and dated 1803 was sold in December 1969 by King and Chasemore for 490 guineas; and a month earlier one with its mount bearing the 1840 hallmark sold for 460 guineas.

Agate snuff-boxes are often unrecognised and may be bought for a few shillings. A gold-mounted example of cartouche form with the cover and base each set with a mocha stone agate, and attributed to about 1740, was sold by Christies for 180 guineas in June 1970. A less attractive oval example cut from solid striated agate and gold mounted, dating to about 1800, sold for 50 guineas. A gold mounted onyx bordered with chased flowers and foliage and engine-turned sides, by Charles Rawlings, London, hallmarked in 1823, made 340 guineas.

The knowledgeable collector of pre-1780 pinchbeck distinguishes this metal at a glance from gilded brass. Bargains have been possible for some dealers class such boxes as brass and fine examples have been sold for a matter of shillings. Yet Christies obtained 90 guineas for a rectangular example with bombé sides and a cover set with a jasper ware plaque.

Mother of pearl snuff-boxes with silver mounts and lids painted with scenes command prices ranging between 20 and 50 guineas, but plain early Victorian examples are to be had at a fraction of these prices.

In June 1970 many Staffordshire enamel snuff-boxes of the late 18th century appeared on the market including a rectangular example painted in colours with flower sprays within *bianco sopra bianco* scroll cartouches and trellis work, with mounts of gilded metal. Measuring $2\frac{1}{4}$ in. wide, this sold for 32 guineas. Two ovals $3\frac{1}{2}$ and 4 in. wide sold for 40 guineas each. A fine Battersea enamel snuff-box, bought in the late 1920s for £2, its approximate retail value at the time of manufacture, sold for 600 guineas. Collectors unfamiliar with this branch of English craftsmanship should inspect and handle some of the fine enamel snuff-boxes in our national museums and beware of reproductions.

Common snuff-boxes in poor condition are valued at no more than £2 each. For instance, a plain surfaced Sheffield plate snuff-box with a badly worn lid revealing large areas of copper was seen in Canterbury priced at £7. It would have been an expensive purchase at more than a pound.

*Art and Antiques Weekly* in the issue dated 18 July 1970 illustrated a Georgian horn snuff mull. A photograph had been submitted to five provincial dealers for their estimates of its retail value. The prices given ranged from £9 to £30.

# CHAPTER 2

# Snuff Rasps and their Cases:
# Spoons: Handkerchiefs

## SNUFF RASPS AND THEIR CASES

MOST SOCIAL customs prompt the development of a highly personalised art of their own. When snuff-taking was transformed from a plebeian indulgence into a fashionable accomplishment by the 1690s, the snuff rasped by dealers from carottes of tobacco tended to be adulterated with titillating pepper, touch wood or one of the sternutatory herbs. This established a need for personal snuff-rasps so that snuff-takers could grind their own powder direct from a carrot-shaped plug of tightly rolled tobacco leaves. These would have been soaked in one of several spiced oils, providing snuff connoisseurs with a range of flavours that successfully masked the bad breath prevalent at the time and was a pungent protection against ill odours. The plug, known as a carotte from early in the 17th century, was drawn a few times over the sharp, jagged teeth of the silver or steel rasp, providing a supply of powdered snuff to be carried in the snuff-box so that a pinch of the powder could be placed on the back of the hand and sniffed up the nose. This freshly prepared snuff was known by its French name *tabac râpé*. The term, anglicised as 'rappee', was long applied to a coarse, inexpensive snuff made from darker, unoiled tobacco leaves.

Of necessity the sharp teeth of the rasp had to be protected by a case or cover of silver, ivory or a wood such as box-wood, walnut or pear-wood which soon became an accepted detail among a gentleman's toilet accessories. Length ranged between about seven and twelve inches, but there were diminutive three-inch rasps, too, for the pocket, kept in wear-resistant cases of leather or embroidered cloth.

The best of these snuff rasps, now splendidly patinated, have become collectors' treasures. Their convex covers may be exquisitely decorated with all-over patterns. The silver may be tooled in relief embossments, the ivory carved, the wood carved or inlaid with ivory or exotic woods of contrasting colour. Some are brightly japanned. Dean Swift recorded in 1711 that he ground his snuff on a rasp fitting into an ivory case.

Subjects for rasp case ornament included the period's favourite Old Testament stories such as Susannah and the Elders and nude figures under the guise of classical tableaux as well as sporting motifs, coats of arms and cyphers and numerous formal patterns. Many cases were designed and made in France. Indeed, some collectors claim that snuff-rasp cases were not made in England. This is contradicted by the fact that they were entered in the 1737 price list of the London Assay Office, the cost of assay being one penny each. Hall-marked examples are recorded.

Silver rasp cases made between 1697 and 1720 were in high standard silver, the hallmarks including the figure of Britannia and the lion's head erased, instead of the leopard's head and lion passant of sterling silver. Only the case was hallmarked: the rasp itself contained more than the legal proportion of copper in order to make the silver harder, springier and long-wearing under daily rasping.

Three styles of personal snuff rasp are to be found: (1) with pivoting cover; (2) with sliding cover; (3) with the rasp fully exposed, needing the protection of a leather case.

In the pivoting design the thin cover was flat and tapering on plan, swivelling on a joint at the wide end. When swung open the cover disclosed the perforated rasp of heavily alloyed silver, iron or steel. At the back of the rasp, to receive the snuff, the silver casing was sunk in a shallow recess with a thin raised rib down its centre. This prevented the rasp from sagging with use and provided two channels for the snuff to flow without clogging from under the rasp at the narrow end and neatly into the snuff-box.

The rasp case, consisting of a sliding shutter concealing the iron rasp, was a narrow rectangle, often with a rounded end. This might be shaped as a scallop shell on each face and covered a small recess into which the powdered snuff was collected from beneath the rasp. More often, however, the end was plainly rounded with a spout from which the snuff was poured into the pocket snuff-box. The rasp was fitted over a fixed back, somewhat rounded to form a long shallow rectangular recess. The shutter that covered it was arranged to slide lengthwise between a pair of grooves and was ornamented with an all-over design matched by that of the rounded back. The exposed type of rasp was merely a grater set into a shallow wooden receptacle shaped to catch the falling snuff.

Mill-ground tobacco snuff appears to have been marketed in bulk no earlier than 1702 when Admiral Sir George Rooke captured from Spanish vessels near Cadiz several thousand barrels of Spanish snuff and a further large cargo of Havana snuff in Vigo Bay. This was distributed throughout the country by sailors who received it in lieu of prize money. Known as Vigo snuff and sold at cheap rates it set the seal on the use of tobacco snuff by the poorer members of the community. From as early as about 1715 the use of personal rasps steadily declined although in 1760 such an individualist as Dr Johnson still preferred to rasp his own rappee, having discovered that the factory-milled product might be adulterated with chicory leaves steeped in tar oil. Some continued the custom to as late as the end of the century.

As snuff-takers turned more and more to factory milled and blended snuff sold under brand names, this meant that the main demand for rasps was among the more exclusive retailers who ground special snuffs and concocted personal blends. The rasps they used were bat-shaped instruments about a foot long. As the black-boy was the tobacconist's shop sign so this style of rasp became the snuff-seller's distinguishing symbol.

The trade card of Fribourg & Treyer, 'at the Rasp & Crown, upper End of Ye Hay Market, London', issued during the 1730s illustrates such a snuff rasp. This was a board tapering from a width of about six inches to four inches with a short handle at the narrow end. The centre was chisel-sunk leaving a narrow rim into which an iron grater was fitted, space being allowed beneath to catch the grated tobacco. This was poured into a mortar and ground to an impalpable powder with a pestle. Snuff-men sold carottes to their customers and charged for rasping. In 1765 Lord Spencer bought '1 Paris carotte £1.1.0; Rasping 1.0; Cannister 6d'.

By the mid-18th century snuff-sellers preferred a rasp in the shape of a half-cylinder fitted into a silver frame with a semi-circular handle. This resembled a kitchen grater and measured from four to ten inches in length, with the top and bottom ends covered, the lower end being hinged to permit removal of the snuff. The frame might have gadrooned rims with a reeded handle. In another design a cylindrical steel grater was set in a silver frame, the side pieces continuing over the top to form a semi-circular handle.

The Sheffield platers in the 1770s evolved a new design in domestic snuff rasps. This measured about a foot in length and had a shallow, flat-based oval body. Two-thirds of this was covered by a convex rasp fitted into a hinged frame. The remainder consisted of a box to hold the unused portion of the carotte.

The rough surface of the rasp consisted of a series of small raised protuberances roughly broken from behind with a steel tool shaped to give them a jagged edge. For silver cases the rasp was of heavily alloyed silver hammered until springy and tough. In about 1740 the sheet iron rasp came into use. This was usually framed in silver to lie snugly within the body of the box, resting upon a ledge formed by a narrow ribbon of silver encircling the interior of the rim. Hammered sheet iron was used until the 1720s when the more efficient, longer-wearing rolled steel came into use. This was thinly tinned to prevent rust, which friction of the tobacco in fact quickly removed. French plating with silver leaf was even less permanent.

From the early 1790s the rolled steel used for snuff rasps was annealed in a bed of hot charcoal about two feet deep, the lower part of the fire being in a state of incandescence, the upper layer at a lower temperature. This caused a condition suitable for the development of oxide colours. After removal from the fire the steel was hardened by being plunged into raw whale oil and then vigorously rubbed with an oil-soaked pad of beaver felt. This process surfaced the steel with a hard blue film capable of resisting the friction of the tobacco. Rasps from this period are always in excellent condition. In the early rasp the jagged-edge piercings were irregularly spaced and appear to have been forced into the metal by means of a sharp punch. Later the perforations were made by raising small hemispheres with a fly-press in such a way as to leave a perfectly flat ground; each hemisphere was then broken by a tool, leaving a jagged edge.

Makers of snuff rasps bought graters by the sheet which they cut to fit their rasp cases or frames, for many a rasp shows severed perforations around the edge.

### SNUFF-SPOONS

Many women snuff-takers snuffed from a tiny spoon or nose shovel of sterling silver, often gilded. This fashionably super-seded the more commonly used quill. Spoon and quill kept the nails clean and the custom also meant that the fastidious woman could proffer her personal box with little risk of its coming into direct contact with her fellow snuffer's fingers.

Snuff-spoons or ladles seldom weighed more than five penny-weights and were therefore exempt from hallmarking. The spoon was commonly about 2 in. long with a shallow oval bowl; some bowls were hemispherical and others shaped like shovels. A snuff-spoon was usually included among the fitments of an 18th-century etui and was also an accompaniment of the table snuff-box.

### SNUFF-HANDKERCHIEFS

Fashion required that after snuffing one hand and the upper lip should be dusted with a ceremonial handkerchief measuring from 18 in. to 24 in. square. An advertisement in the *London Gazette*, 1694, described a sophisticated snuff-handkerchief as being 'in lawn with a broad rim, laced around with fine lace about four fingers broad'. When the fashion for snuff-taking snowballed during Queen Anne's reign it brought into use more serviceable cambric and cotton handkerchiefs known as snuff-napkins. These might also be spread to protect the neck-cloth, shirt and waistcoat from falling snuff. At this time men's coat tails began to be fitted with capacious pockets in which to carry the bulky snuff-napkin. It was from these loosely hanging pockets that pickpockets for the next hundred years found fine game, extracting lawn and other expensive handkerchiefs for which there was a ready receiver's market. Those who specialised in diving into coat pockets for sneezers, skins and dummies (snuff-boxes, purses and pocket-books) were known as tail-buzzers. Women carried their snuff-handkerchiefs in linen pockets sewn to straps encircling their waists between the petticoats. It became a fashionable ostentation to carry in the hand an elaborately worked laced handkerchief, the pocket concealing a cotton square for actual use.

Obviously the snuffer called for coloured handkerchiefs, the less to reveal the scant laundering of personal linen in a day of heavily taxed soap. Some were dyed a light brown tint in an effort to disguise snuff stains; others were ornamented with simple wood block printing in bright colours. To protect the decaying wool trade, textile printers were forbidden by law from 1720 to 1774 to use material made entirely of cotton but even then the production of plain blue cotton snuff-handkerchiefs was permitted. Squares of silk began to be used for the first time in 1721.

When the technique of monochrome copper-plate printing began to be applied to textiles in the early 1750s a demand was created for snuff-handkerchiefs illustrating pictorial scenes, first on silk, then on a fabric woven with a linen warp and a cotton weft and from 1774 on cotton. The introduction of Arkwright's water-power loom at this time enabled calico to be woven with a smooth, regular surface upon which clear designs were reproduced in delicate detail.

The only permanent colours so far were black and reddish purple. Printing in red was evolved in about 1800; blue and green a few years later. From about 1815 stippling replaced dark mottled shadow-work in pictures which now displayed more roundly modelled three-dimensional effects.

In 1831 the drastic excise duties long imposed on calico printing were removed. From 1718 a tax of threepence a square yard had been levied on the calico manufacturer and a further threepence upon the printer. From 1782 the printer's tax had been increased to fifteen per cent of the fabric's value, increased to twenty per cent in 1812.

So far snuff-handkerchiefs had been printed singly by hand presses: roller machinery had been invented half a century earlier but was unsuitable for all-over picture work on snuff-handkerchiefs. Steam-driven and enlarged roller machinery now came into use, printing monochrome handkerchiefs at the rate of 9,000 a day, equal to the production of 42 hand-presses. Four standard sizes were made: 21, 24½, 28 and 31½ in. square.

Adaptations to the printing machine during the 1840s made it possible to print snuff-handkerchiefs in black and three shades of four colours – a total of thirteen tint variations. These were later augmented by superimposing one colour over another. Silk and lawn handkerchiefs had long been hemmed by hand-sewing. Cotton handkerchiefs were rarely hemmed until after the invention of the lock-stitch sewing machine in 1851.

The collector of snuff-handkerchiefs will find that they offer vivid glimpses into the pleasures and enthusiasms of their period. They depict a wide variety of portraits and contemporaneous events. Subjects range from popular views of celebrated buildings to representations of the willow pattern. Those printed with such betrothal motifs as hearts and love birds, or with amatory pictures and couplets, were known as flirting squares. Snuff-handkerchiefs will be found bearing the insignia of Orange clubs and Masonry; Niagara Falls with explanatory details; the coronations of George IV, William IV and Queen Victoria. Crimean handkerchiefs dated 1855 embody maxims for a soldier, army signalling, medals for distinguished conduct and long service, the music of bugle calls, and pictures of events in the field.

From 1842 to 1883 it was possible to register industrial designs at the Patent Office, giving protection from industrial piracy for three years upon payment of a fee of one pound. Such a registered picture contained in some inconspicuous place, usually incorporated in the design itself, a diamond-shaped registration mark containing symbols from which the name of the printer may be interpreted by Patent Office officials.

Although calico printers in the 1870s tried to save a declining trade with new effects produced by recently invented synthetic dyes, printed handkerchiefs were issued only as souvenirs, on commemorative occasions, for propaganda purposes, and with illustrated nursery rhymes for children.

# CHAPTER 3

# Gold: Silver: Miniatures

## GOLD

WHEN Beau Nash delighted fashionable Bath with his snuff-boxes of jewelled gold, similar bijouterie had already scintillated for more than thirty years at the Court of France. But now, in the reign of Queen Anne, the English goldsmith began his own contributions to this work, creating snuff-boxes for men and women in precious metals. The English jeweller was particularly in his element designing splendidly proportioned, delicately ornamented and superbly finished boxes in gold and silver, now a joy to the modern collector. Details were considered meticulously. Lids were made to fit tightly yet open smoothly. This important feature was recorded in *Pandora's Box*, 1719:

> *Charming in shape, with polish't rays of light,*
> *A joint so fine it shuns the sharpest light.*

The hinge, too, was made with watch-maker's precision, extending the full width of the rectangular lid. In the oval shape, opening lengthwise, the hinge was positioned about one-fifth of the distance from each end of the box and here, too, joints were virtually invisible. Hinges were external and riveted to the back: not until the 1740s was the integral hinge in regular use. Constant working of an ill-made hinge eventually wore the lugs, causing the lid to become loose and let snuff leak into the pocket. Even the slightest projection of the thumb-lift on the front of the lid was a hazard seldom introduced to pocket boxes intended for snuff, since the projection might catch against the clothing when being lifted from the pocket and spill the powder.

Thumb-lifts when used might be designed and ornamented to match the overall decoration or set with diamonds, sprays of

3

flowers always being fashionable. The existence of the slightest
defect in a gold snuff-box of the Georgian period should arouse
suspicion regarding its genuineness. The early gold snuff-box
was engagingly slender to fit the waistcoat pocket.

Circular snuff-boxes were fashionable, too, at first with
hinged lids. From about 1720 circular lids might be of the pull-
off pattern. These were made until the end of the century despite the hazard of a jerky movement spilling the snuff. Gold
boxes with pull-off lids were more commonly used as containers
for breath-sweetening comfits, aromatic sponge or patches – but
to collectors 'snuff-box' has become the generic term. When
fitted with hinged lids, such boxes are often difficult to distinguish from true snuff-boxes, but minor characteristics, such as a
mirror in a patch box lid, may make this possible.

Jewelled boxes of the Queen Anne period had rounded
corners: the oval shape, however, outnumbered circular boxes
during the reigns of the first two Georges (1714–1760).
Engraved trade cards in the British Museum illustrate many
ovals, mostly with curved sides, from about 1725 to the late
1760s. Shallow rectangular boxes with rounded corners were
also fashionable at this time. Base and cover were encircled with
plain moulding, ornament being restricted to the cover.
Irregular shapes were numerous too, some designed with an
escallop shell outline, others, from 1727, as asymmetrical
cartouches.

Until about 1715 lid decoration consisted mainly of engraved
armorials or cyphers, sometimes with a colourful hardstone or
shell as a central feature. The *Daily Courant* referred in 1705 to a
gold snuff-box decorated 'with a large blue onyx stone upon the
lid'. Such snuff-boxes were specifically exempted from assay after
1739: examples struck with hall-marks earlier than this date are
extremely rare. Classic decoration in relief became fashionable
on gold snuff-boxes with the accession of George I. These were
low-chased on matt grounds, allegorical scenes and heroic
subjects being usual. The relief work became higher from about
1730 and had become customary by the mid-1760s.

Georgian snuff-boxes in gold from about 1760 until 1815 were usually rectangular and from the 1790s the sides tended to be concave or rounded in *bombé* form rather than vertical, depth varying between ¾ in. and 1¼ in. The pointed oval or shuttle shape was a late 18th-century fashion but has proved less enduring than the straight-hinged rectangle. Although these were the prevailing shapes, no real classification is possible for every geometrical and curved shape was approved and goldsmiths worked with freedom of form, material, colour and decoration. During the second half of the century it was customary for winter snuff-boxes to be heavy and those carried during the summer months to be light-weight. Jewelled and lavishly worked boxes were protected from damage with fitted cases, shagreen, ivory and morocco leather always being fashionable.

Many handsome snuff-boxes were bedecked with gold of various hues, as many as four different alloys enriching a single design such as a bouquet in vari-coloured gold in relief against an engine-turned ground, with borders and corners similarly decorated. Golds shaded to blue and green tones against a background of yellow gold were particularly fashionable, with burnished highlights. Silver oxide added to 22-carat gold produced a green alloy; copper oxide, red; and iron oxide, a bluish tint.

A magnificent series of gold snuff-boxes elaborately chased on cover and sides was made early in the George III period. In these the goldsmith patterned the metal by applying various punches to the outer surface. In *repoussé* work the embossed design was raised from the underside. Less common were boxes decorated with *ciselé* work in which the metal was carved as though it were wood. These three styles of ornament, with the addition of engraving, might decorate a single snuff-box.

With the assistance of artist enamellers, London goldsmiths produced some spectacular snuff-boxes decorated with portraits and other paintings upon the gold ground, which enhanced the brilliance of the enamel colours. Others were set with gold plaques displaying pictures commissioned from independent artist enamellers. *Basse-taille* enamelling, seldom seen on English snuff-boxes, consists of cutting designs into the surface of the gold and filling the channels with translucent enamels through which the engraved lines are visible.

Panels of gouache and grisaille painting are to be found set in snuff-box lids. *Gouache* is a term for painting in water colours rendered opaque by the addition of white and gum. The result is a velvety surface reflecting light. *Grisaille* is a term for painting in soft tones of grey, causing solid bodies to be represented as if in relief. *Verre églomisé* decoration on panels of glass set in the lid and sides of early Georgian snuff-boxes is uncommon. This ornament consists of gold or silver foil on the underside of the glass against a ground of red, green or, more often, blue.

Portraits originally held a personal interest only, the sitters for the most part being now unknown. A portrait of a celebrity is usually indication that the box was a gift from the person portrayed. This might be a miniature painted on ivory, often protected by a convex glass. Such ornament is rarely found inside the lid as dust would obscure its delicate lines. The snuff-box intended only for display in a cabinet usually contains a portrait, sometimes a pair of a husband and wife. Celebrities displayed magnificent collections, most of them received as gifts and often inscribed within the lid.

The *tabatière secrète* has a miniature portrait painted on ivory concealed beneath the central ornament of the cover. This is revealed by pressing a secret spring. Others have an erotic painting hidden in this space. In some combined snuff and patch boxes the patches were carried in the small cavity.

From about 1815 gold and silver were used more lavishly than during the years of the Napoleonic wars, heavy castings in high relief superseding the more delicate hand-craftsmanship. This brought about a change in mood: expressed, for example, in the vogue for snuff-box lids displaying scenes adapted from Dutch paintings. These castings were, of course, surface finished by hand-carving and were sometimes set within mounts of gold.

In the majority of instances the framing was cast too. The lid design might incorporate a tiny central escutcheon upon which the owner's crest or cypher was engraved.

Birmingham became the main centre for the manufacture of gold snuff-boxes and, like the London goldsmiths, specialised in engine-turned ornament during the first third of the 19th century. The sides of the fashionable box were concave, usually with surfaces engine-turned in a single matching pattern. Panels of differing designs decorated a long series of gold snuff-boxes during the 1820s. Wide mounts with flower and foliage decoration in deep relief were the rule: the oak leaf and acorn pattern was popular long after the end of the Napoleonic wars in 1815.

The lid at this period might be set with a cast and chased scene of hunting or other sport. Presentation boxes in gold were elaborately designed, the goldsmith preparing a master drawing illustrating the plan and side views. Several copies might be made.

No further development occurred in the design of gold snuff-boxes until 1854 when the great volume of imported jewellery in heavily alloyed gold urged the Goldsmiths' Company to agitate for a change in the regulations. For the first time in England jewellers were permitted to make use of compound metals, that is, the gold was alloyed. Until 1798 no quality other than 22-carat gold was passed by the Assay Office. The two per cent alloy in this, normally copper, accounts for the reddish tint displayed by gold snuff-boxes made before that year.

The new qualities included 18-carat from 1798: that is, 18 parts gold and six of alloy which might be copper, copper and silver, or copper, silver and zinc. Three differing tints then faced the purchaser of an 18-carat snuff-box, only 75 per cent of which was actually gold. The term *carat* indicates the proportion of gold and not a definite unit of weight as in precious stones. From 1854 snuff-boxes were made in 15-carat gold; in 12-carat consisting of equal parts of gold and alloy; and 9-carat containing 15 parts alloy to nine of gold. Only by long usage of the term can this quality be termed gold, but legally this is permitted. These four standards are indicated by numerals stamped at the assay office. The price of 22-carat gold remained constant at about 84s an ounce throughout the gold snuff-box period.

### SILVER

Silver snuff-boxes constitute the most numerous group available to collectors, dating as they do from the reign of Charles II to late in that of Victoria. The precious metal has been preserved: those of base metal and the like for the most part have been destroyed. Chronological classification by form alone is impossible: for instance identical patterns were made during early Georgian and early Victorian periods. Hallmarks, of course, serve the purpose of accurate dating, but frequently the slight continual friction against a chamois-lined pocket has worn the silver until marks have become indecipherable. In dating such pieces reliance must be placed upon methods of craftsmanship and associated ornament.

Few silver snuff-boxes remain that were made earlier than about 1730, but London newspapers of the period record numerous descriptions in the columns advertising lost and stolen goods. The two examples quoted here are taken from among a hundred or more collated from various sources. *The London Gazette*, September 1692, refers to 'a Silver Snuff-Box Guilt on the inside, and the top of it is Engraven with a Cypher and a Garter round it, and a Duke's Coronet'. This style of decoration is characteristic of the period. Silver snuff-boxes might be lavishly decorated, however. *The Daily Courant*, September 1709, described such a stolen example: 'Silver Snuff-Box, on the Lid a Locket compos'd of 10 Garnetts, in the middle an old-fashioned Chrystal under which 2 Angels support a Crown over a Cypher, at each corner of the Box on the same side is set 4 Escallope Shells at the Tail of each Escallope four Stones.' The lid of a two-inch oval snuff-box made by the celebrated Thomas Isod which I recently examined was exquisitely engraved in the limited space with two Comedy figures miming to music against an architectural background with a surround of shells, scrolling foliage and caryatids.

Most snuff-boxes of the early 18th century were constructed from sections of plate flattened from the ingot by the hand-hammer and hard-soldered together and burnished so that seams were invisible. Much more costly was the snuff-box hand-raised from the silver plate as a single unit and fitted with a hinged flat lid composed of a single piece of plate. Shallow circular snuff-boxes were turned in the lathe from solid castings and fitted with hinged lids. Some boxes in each group were given cast lids.

The silver used between 1697 and 1720 was by law required to be of the quality known as high or Britannia standard, containing less alloy and consequently softer than sterling. For this reason the plate was slightly thicker than in boxes of sterling silver. The assay office mark included a figure of Britannia in place of the lion passant gardant, indication of sterling quality.

Georgian silversmiths continued to use hand-beaten plate, but by the 1770s the factory silver refiners and rollers of Sheffield and Birmingham were supplying rolled plate at lower prices and this could be shaped in the press. Circular snuff-boxes began to be spun in the lathe. Small master silversmiths bought snuff-box units from the factories and finished and assembled them in their own workshops. In the early 19th century snuff-boxes were made from rolled plate virtually concealed beneath heavy ornamental castings or rose engine-turning.

In Georgian work topical embossments were fashionable, particularly portrait busts of naval and military heroes and, less commonly, political figures. The Jacobites tended to carry snuff-boxes embossed or engraved with portraits of Prince Charles, the Jacobite rose and other emblems associated with the intrigues around 1745. Hallmarks show these to have been made in Scotland in about 1750; some later examples bear the maker's mark of Collin, a silversmith of Bond Street, London. As with other Stuart mementoes, however, the collector has to be on the watch for Victorian boxes, including the box claiming a cover of oak wood from the famous tree of Boscobel, framed in silver appropriately engraved with the future Charles II peeping from among foliage.

Oval snuff-boxes outnumbered other shapes in silver until the 1760s and displayed almost every variety of ornament apart from precious stones. Trade cards now in the British Museum depict ovals, mostly with curved sides, from about 1725 to 1760, the single exception being a rectangle of about 1750. Rectangular snuff-boxes were made with rounded or canted corners: they were very shallow, some but $\frac{3}{8}$ in. deep. In such a design the lid and base corners were encircled with plain strengthening moulding and ornament was restricted to the top. This might be engraved on the outside with a coat of arms in an expansive ornamental cartouche, or the outside might be entirely plain and a picture engraved within the lid. Irregular shapes were numerous too, some designed on the escallop shell outline, with straight hinges. Among other lid treatments of the period was the casting in all-over high relief of an intricate figure scene, usually adapted from a well-known painting and enclosed within borders. This was finished by hand-carving. Alternatively, cast ornament, chased and burnished, might be applied to a lid, or a raised design might be achieved with embossing and chasing in an intricate all-over pattern. Such effects contrasted with the flat formality of other patterns in rose engine-turning. This formal patterning was widely acceptable over almost a century, the box being ornamented on all six surfaces. The slight roughness in texture prevented the box from slipping accidentally through the fingers and was less easily marred than plain silver by constant handling.

The interior of the silver snuff-box was gilded to prevent discolouring of the metal by the snuff and its added flavouring ingredients. The gold remained brilliantly radiant, a perfect ground against which to offer a pinch of snuff. Embossed lids and sides were lined with gilded plate to prevent accumulation of snuff in the interior recesses created by such ornament. There was a late 18th-century vogue for lining silver snuff-boxes with a thin veneer of highly polished tortoiseshell.

For a time, through the 1760s–80s, comparatively few silver snuff-boxes were made. This was due in part to the popularity of colourful boxes in painted enamels, then at their finest, but more especially to the challenge of Sheffield plate, much cheaper and difficult to distinguish at a glance from sterling silver. The London silversmiths met this competition by loading snuff-boxes with styles of ornament impossible with Sheffield plate: even the shape was a challenge as the rectangular box became boldly rounded in a manner that would render Sheffield plate especially vulnerable to copper-revealing wear.

Regarding other shapes, the octagonal snuff-box had been fashionable from 1690 to the 1740s. It was usually small, about two inches wide, with the lid all-over engraved. Triangular snuff-boxes had a mid 18th-century vogue. They were usually given silver-gilt mounts with lid and base set with hardstones such as lapis lazuli. Heart-shaped snuff-boxes had flat lids crest-engraved and bordered with engraved bands of appropriate scrollwork. These were invariably shallow.

The snuff-box with a sea-shell as a container, its edge cut and fitted with a silver mount, usually reeded, achieved some popularity between about 1790 and the 1830s. Cowrie shells were in considerable use for this purpose. The lid hinged near to the wide end of the shell opening with a thumb-lift near the point. The lid was usually engraved with a wide border of swags and festoons, or foliate scrolls with a central cartouche containing a cypher. Sizes ranged from $3\frac{1}{2}$ in. to 2 in. long. Cypraea shells were also used. Hallmarks suggest that such snuff-boxes were made at the coastal towns of Newcastle, Arbroath and Cork.

The early 19th-century tendency to use silver lavishly and replace costly hand labour with heavy casting was expressed even on snuff-boxes. There was a marked change of mood, but snuff-boxes escaped the disastrous excesses of some table silver. There was, for example, a vogue for snuff-boxes displaying scenes adapted from Dutch oil paintings. Such ornament, cast in high relief and chased, was held in a rim shaped from flat plate which was fashionably engine-turned. In another series the cast frames constituted the major ornament. A plain box made from rolled plate had wide, boldly convex moulding soldered around the lid and covering the sides entirely. The lid might be engine-turned with a central reserve containing an engraved scene, often of a religious nature, or a commemorative motif or inscription. At this time the standard lid decoration might incorporate a tiny rectangle for the owner's crest or cypher.

During the first one-third of the 19th century the lid of a silver-gilt snuff-box made in London or Birmingham might be set with a solid gold plaque upon which a crest, cypher or presentation inscription might be engraved without revealing the fact that the box was basically of sterling silver. The border might be composed of a design of applied vine tendrils on a matted ground and the sides and base engine-turned before gilding.

Many sporting snuff-boxes are associated with the early 19th century. A typical design had rounded corners and projecting rims, the sides vertical and engine-turned, the lid of flat plate displaying an applied cast and chased scene or motif in silhouette, such as a horse or greyhound, with a ribbon above for the animal's name and another below for the occasion and date. Pocket snuff-boxes were also engraved with scenes of prize-fighting and the like.

Silver has always proved particularly amenable for use in combination with more colourful materials. Throughout the period under review jewel-encrusted gold snuff-boxes had their less ostentatious counterparts in boxes of silver-gilt set with gemstones such as emeralds, garnets and amethysts and variegated hardstones. The top and base might be of carved stone and the sides of the box elaborately embossed or cast in relief and chased.

Cheap, pressed light-weight snuff-boxes for ladies were made in numerous shapes and forms: they might be round, oval, octagonal, irregular in outline, or represent hearts, purses, escallop shells, travelling chests, shoes or books. The lids of a long series of post-1815 snuff-boxes were pressed with a range of views of castles, abbeys, national buildings, stately homes. One authority has collated more than 700 such views and states that nine out of ten are struck with the anchor of the Birmingham Assay Office. Makers' marks include those of Nathaniel Mills, Joseph Taylor, John Shaw, Samuel Pemberton, Thomas Willmore, George Bettridge, William Pugh and Joseph Phillimore.

The silver harnessing technique was applied to snuff-boxes from about 1830. The box, carved from colourful hardstone, was hammered with chased silver openwork in an all-over design of birds, animals, flowers, foliage and elaborate scroll-work, so that the lively metalwork and the stone immensely enhanced each other. By the late 1840s birds and other motifs might be set with innumerable tiny glittering gem-stones.

Snuff-boxes of oxidised silver appeared during the late 1840s, ornamented with handsome pictorial relief work. These bas reliefs were electrotypes. Two such boxes with sporting scenes were seen at the Great Exhibition, 1851: a Scottish deer stalker and an angler with a catch of fish on a line.

In the early snuff-box a touch on a small stud operating a catch allowed the lid to open. In the early 18th century it was found that a thumb-lift attached to the front edge of the lid mount was safer and more reliable in its action. These thumb-lifts varied from a narrow plain scroll flange to a wide cast plate with an ornamented upper surface, such as a floral design or scroll and shell.

### MINIATURES

Miniature portraits painted in full colour were fashionable ornament on the lids of gold and gilded silver snuff-boxes throughout the 18th century. These pictures, usually the work of expert craftsmen rather than original artists, were painted in water colours, at first on vellum and later on oval slips of ivory which imparted a delicate lustre to the carnation or flesh areas.

The system of painting followed by the majority of early miniaturists was described in *The Art of Painting in Miniature*, 1735. The portraits were painted on vellum stiffened by pasting it to a plate of copper, brass or wood. 'This pasting must be on the Edges of your Velom only and behind the plate; For which purpose your Velom must exceed your Plate. The Part you paint upon must never be pasted . . . there must be a clean white Paper between the Velom and the Plate.' The collector should inspect a miniature that has a metal table to ensure that it has been flattened by the battery method, a point sometimes overlooked by the modern copyist. In copies, too, the paper between the vellum and the plate may be omitted. Until the 1720s miniature painters prepared their own colours from ingredients sold by apothecaries. By 1730, however, fifteen suitable colours could be bought from the print shops for painting 'portraits in little', as miniatures were then called.

The use of thin ivory tablets for this work was introduced to England by Bernard Lens junior (1682–1740) in 1708, but was confined to leading artists until the 1740s. The old ivories were not polished, in fact it was common for the painting surface to be slightly roughened to ensure that the colours would bite. Before use the miniaturist rubbed this surface with garlic juice.

The Georgian miniaturist began by dead-colouring the whole area of the portrait, laying on the paint with smooth clear strokes of a pencil brush. The base for faces consisted of white which was mixed with a tinge of blue for women, vermillion for men, and a little ochre to suggest age. Over this ground the portrait was dotted or stippled. Some miniaturists made round dots and others preferred longish flecks. Those to whom speed of production was important used hatching, that is, short strokes crossing each other in every direction: obviously such portraits tended to be inferior.

Collectors may find snuff-boxes set with miniatures within the lids and, in some instances, portraying a member of the original owner's family. But they should be aware of the fact that forgeries have been abundant for the past seventy years: in 1903 fraudulent Cosways were discussed in an art journal. One may find a miniature set in a snuff-box of an earlier period, or even an antique miniature set on the lid of a much later box. An example from Horace Walpole's Strawberry Hill collection was described in the sale catalogue, lot 101, as '*a fine gold escallop shaped* SNUFF BOX, richly enamelled with flowers, on the top a very fine miniature of James I by Hilliard, and within a portrait of Queen Elizabeth, also by Hilliard, both in the finest manner of this much admired artist, the onyx at the bottom of the box is considered perfectly unique'. These miniatures were painted on the plain backs of playing cards.

The most fashionable painter of miniatures for setting in radiantly bejewelled snuff-boxes of George III's day was Richard Cosway, RA (1742–1821). Ivory played a great part in the success of his technique which allowed it to gleam through the very thinly applied water-colours with remarkable brilliance: in many instances one may note areas of its surface bearing no trace of colour, the curve of the cheek or the rounded flesh of the shoulders and bosom being the creamy ivory itself. He persistently used a cold, clear, bright ultramarine. Early and late grounds are distinguished by a greyish-green tint; work of his middle period by grounds of mottled white or grey. One of his characteristics was his treatment of hair in washes of colour touched with delicate lines and suggesting masses rather than wiry detail. Some of his most exquisite portraits are found in the lids of jewelled snuff-boxes and painted directly on box-lids of ivory.

The Georgian painters whose miniature portraits are found set in snuff-box lids were a numerous group. High among them are the following, but about thirty others were of comparable ability.

*Gervase Spencer* (d. 1763) painted excellent portraits of which **Horace Walpole** wrote: 'He greatly favoured a very pale blue background, but substituted for it sometime a dull brown colour.' His water-colour effects display an unusual clarity of definition.

*Jeremiah Meyer*, RA (1735–89), miniaturist to George III and Queen Charlotte, worked on ivory with transparent water-colours. His draughtsmanship tended towards the angular, the entire surface of the ivory being covered with very fine lines, long and short, and crossing each other at all angles to secure adequate face modelling. These lines are often so fine that it is difficult to see them without a glass. Unfortunately he used a fading flesh-tint.

*John Smart* (1741–1811) is known by the incomparable textures of his flesh tints in a colour used by no other miniaturist.

*Ozias Humphry*, RA (1742–1810) usually painted three-quarter face against a background of green, brown or blue, and gave his sitter long, narrow eyes resulting in a sleepy expression.

*Samuel Shelley* (1753–1808) was a devotee of pale colours and had the personal characteristic of sometimes turning his ovals so that width was greater than height, ideal for certain snuff-boxes.

*George Engleheart* (1752–1824) is known for his rigidly accurate drawing, and some rich dark cross-hatching on the feminine neck and shoulders.

*Andrew Plimer* (1757–1822) duplicated Cosway's technique but substituted line work for fleecy hair masses.

*John Couler* (1768–1805), the first artist to exhibit miniatures at the Royal Academy, was notable for the exquisite delicacy of his portraits on snuff-box ivories.

Many of the more splendid of the Georgian snuff-box miniatures were signed with a full name, initials or a monogram: the majority are unsigned. A full signature such as $R^d$ *Cosway* or $Oz^s$ *Humphry* was usually inscribed behind the portrait, between the ivory and the snuff-box lid. The artist's surname might be inscribed on the front of the ivory, but usually no more than a monogram or initials is found in this position. Microscopic in size and mingled among the hair of curls or wig, or concealed in the fold of a dress, these can only be detected after prolonged search with a magnifying glass in a bright light. When gilt or lead pencil has been used it is essential to hold the portrait at the correct angle to the light. A signature may be so close to the edge of the ivory that it is concealed by the encircling mount.

# CHAPTER 4

# Sheffield Plate: Britannia Metal:
# Moiré Metal

## SHEFFIELD PLATE

SNUFF-BOXES were the first articles to be made commercially in Sheffield plate. This important material, superficially resembling silver plate but very much cheaper, consisted of a thin layer of pure silver fused over a thicker layer of copper. The process was invented in 1742 by Thomas Bolsover, Tudor House, Sheffield. A year later he established workshops at Baker Hill, Sheffield, and concentrated on the manufacture of snuff-boxes and buttons.

These boxes were shallow and circular, their lift-off covers measuring about $2\frac{1}{2}$ in. across by $\frac{3}{4}$ in. deep decorated with all-over designs in relief. Early ornament was wholly hand-worked and this style continued throughout the period that these boxes were in vogue – to the late 1770s. But from the 1760s designs were commonly raised in relief by pressing with dies made from the newly invented Huntsman tool steel, harder than any metal made hitherto, and finished by hand chasing.

Covers displayed a wide range of relief patterns such as flowers and foliage among rococo scrollwork, classical scenes with draped figures and elaborate backgrounds, hand-chased portraits of celebrities such as William Pitt, 1st Earl of Chatham and Frederick II of Prussia among a trophy of arms, both in Sheffield City Museum. A style that achieved some popularity consisted of a classical scene pierced and set against a ground of aventurine glass (see p. 93) intended to suggest clouds. Snuff-box bases were stamped beneath with expansive patterns in line-work resembling engraving, such as a basket of fruit surmounted by scrollwork.

The sides of the two units composing the snuff-box were made by encircling each of the decorated discs with a strip of Sheffield plate. The strips were bent into a circle and the ends joined to form rings. The rings were attached to the discs by lapping them over the edges and soldering them into position. Ornamental sides for the box were made by swaging a strip of plate into curved shapes. The seams of the vertical joints are always faintly visible.

Copper at this period could be silver-plated on one side only, the reverse displaying the bare copper. A plain disc of plate, silvered side facing downward, was usually placed within the cover to conceal the copper and to keep the snuff from clogging the undulations caused by the embossments. Examples are to be found with the interior gilded, but others reveal the unplated side of the copper. In some instances the entire interior was lined with highly polished tortoiseshell to prevent oxides forming on the copper and tainting the snuff. The tortoiseshell in the silver might be backed with copper to strengthen it. Copper covered on both sides dates from the late 1760s and is usually found in association with stamped pastoral scenes. The base might consist wholly of a disc of tortoiseshell, its exterior surface engine-turned. A long series of snuff-box covers was set with plaques of tortoiseshell in piqué posé (see p. 118).

The majority of Sheffield plate snuff-boxes from 1760 were rectangular, quite plain and tinned inside. A five-lug hinge extended the full width of the lid. Edges and corners of those now remaining are often pocket-worn revealing a tinge of copper. Oval and circular forms with hinged lids and the pinched rectangle were common. These, from about 1770, might have fluted sides edged with fine plated wire. Oblong snuff-boxes might have rounded ends and were usually fitted with thumb-lifts. Those intended for constant work-a-day use were necessarily of strong plate to prevent warping. From about

4

1780 the cover mount might be set with a skilfully painted Staffordshire enamel.

By this time the majority of Sheffield plate snuff-boxes were of Birmingham manufacture. Sides tended to be concave or rounded in bombé form, depth ranging from $\frac{3}{4}$ in. to $1\frac{1}{4}$ in. The pointed oval or shuttle shape was a vogue of the late 18th and early 19th centuries. None of these shapes has proved as enduring as the plain straight-hinged rectangle.

Matthew Boulton, Soho, Staffordshire, was a prolific maker of snuff-boxes from 1765. In 1767 he wrote to a friend, 'I have lately begun to make snuff-boxes in metal gilt and in tortoiseshell inlaid' – that is piqué posé. He is known to have made circular boxes in Sheffield plate with hinged lids framing panels of exotic woods, mother of pearl and tortoiseshell. Boulton was the first Birmingham maker of Sheffield plate to adapt and bring to perfection silver edges to snuff-boxes, a technique patented in 1785 by Valentine Rawle.

A popular early 19th-century decoration on an otherwise plain snuff-box was a cartwheel copper penny dated 1796, soldered to the centre of the flat lid and close-plated to match the box. The pennies were minted for the Government by Matthew Boulton at Soho and it has been assumed that these boxes were made by his firm, although no marked example has been noted. A second series was made early in the Victorian period by a now anonymous firm who electroplated the pennies.

By careful examination of manufacturing techniques it is possible to attribute an approximate period of manufacture even if shapes and sizes appear to be identical. The double-lapped copper edge dates from 1768; silver-lapped edges were introduced in 1775; narrow cast silver mounts from 1780; silver edges from 1785; bright-cut engraving was first used during the early 1780s and continued until about 1810. Stamped silver mounts filled with lead-tin alloy were introduced in 1790 and wide mounts stamped in silver in about 1815.

To compete with silver boxes the Sheffield plate box might

have to be engraved with a crest or other identifying symbol. To avoid revealing the copper in the engraved lines a shield of more heavily silvered plate might be soldered in, usually in the centre of the lid. By 1810 a silver shield was sweated on over the Sheffield plate on the area of the lid to be engraved. From about 1810 fused silver plate could be rolled appreciably thinner than formerly, cost being perceptibly reduced.

Table snuff-boxes in Sheffield plate, sometimes gilded, were usually circular with lift-off covers and measuring between four and six inches in diameter. An unusual design was spherical, the lower hemisphere supported by a trumpet foot and the upper hemisphere finialled to serve as a lift-off cover.

## BRITANNIA METAL

Concurrently with Sheffield plate snuff-boxes from the 1780s a series of inexpensive snuff-boxes was made from two silvery-looking metals devoid of any coating of silver. These were Vickers white metal and britannia metal, both the invention of James Vickers of Sheffield.

Vickers white metal, dating from the 1770s, is an alloy composed principally of tin with the addition of antimony, copper and bismuth. This alloy so closely resembles sterling silver in colour when new that the casual observer would not be aware of the difference. It is soft and could be cut with a knife. Snuff-boxes in Vickers white metal are rare and those made by the originator are always impressed beneath I. VICKERS in small capitals. The Sheffield Directory for 1787 lists twelve white metal workers.

Early in the 1790s Vickers omitted the bismuth and commercialised this cheaper white alloy under the name of britannia metal. This eventually became very popular, large quantities being made. Brownell's Sheffield Directory of 1817 lists 73 britannia metal makers. Its high silvery lustre with a bluish white tinge was a distinct advance on the current quality of pewter which it superseded. The hardness of britannia metal

made it capable of taking a high polish lost only after a long
period of neglect but then impossible to restore.

Snuff-boxes, following the prevailing silver outlines, were
usually made from thinly rolled metal, bodies and lids being
stamped and fitted with hinged mounts of gilded brass. They
were rarely decorated with more than simple engraving.

Britannia metal continued to be used for snuff-boxes until
about 1850 when it was superseded by electroplated metals.
The vast majority were unmarked. Those made by James
Vickers and his successors between 1806 and 1817 were stamped
on the base I. VICKERS in small capitals and should not be
mistaken for his series in white metal; during the next twenty
years the letters were larger; and after 1837 the small capitals
reappeared with the address BRITANNIA PLACE SHEFFIELD added
below. Other Sheffield makers of marked britannia metal
snuff-boxes included J. Wolstenholme from 1828, P. Ashberry
from 1830, and James Dixon & Sons from 1806, marked
DIXON between that year and 1830.

### MOIRÉ METAL

Snuff-boxes in shapes prevailing during the period 1816 to the
early 1830s were made in moiré metal. Its brilliant surface was
closely covered with stars and other geometrical patterns. The
process of manufacture was patented in 1816 by Edward
Thomason, Birmingham, who had observed that tinned iron
plate held obliquely to the light revealed figured patterns,
particularly on Pontypool tin plates. Impurities were removed
from the surfaces of the snuff-box units by rubbing with nitric
acid and salt. This ensured that the designs would be visible
from every angle. After washing and drying the plate was immediately coated with clear hard varnish to preserve its silvery
brilliance, followed later by several more protective coats and
finally polished by hand.

The small crystalline figures providing this ornament were
obtained by heating the plate until the film of tin melted.

Whilst cooling the coating of tin crystallised into a mass of graceful designs. Variations were achieved by heating only part of the tin. A granite effect resulted from hammering the plate before treating it with nitric acid. This broke the figures into even smaller crystalline patterns.

# CHAPTER 5

# Pinchbeck: Gilt Brass:
# Lancashire Brass

### PINCHBECK

THE NAME of Christopher Pinchbeck (1670–1732) passed into the English language as a synonym for the counterfeit and sham. Yet he was celebrated during his lifetime as the inventor and maker of complicated astronomical clocks, musical automata and church organs. Each year he set up his booth at Bartholomew and Southwark Fairs under the sign of *The Temple of the Muses*, an eye-catching juggler performing on a platform outside. So great was his reputation for melodious devices operated by clockwork that in 1729 his fairground 'Temple' attracted a visit from the Prince and Princess of Wales.

Established originally in St George's Court, Clerkenwell, in 1721 he moved to more central display workrooms in Fleet Street under the sign of *The Astronomico-Musical Clock* with convenient premises nearby. Here he advertised that he made and sold 'Watches of all sorts and Clocks with a variety of musical performers together with a wonderful imitation of several Songs and Voices of an Aviary of Birds so natural that any who saw not the Instrument would be persuaded that it were in Reality what it only represents. He makes musical Automata or Instruments of themselves to play exceedingly well on the Flute, Flaggelet or Organ, Sets of County Dances, Minuets, Jiggs, and the Opera tunes, fit for the diversion of those in places where a Musician is not at Hand. . . . He also Mends Watches and Clocks.'

Pinchbeck's work was mainly for the affluent. In 1722, for instance, he sold an astronomical clock to Sir Robert Walpole

54

for 700 guineas, a musical clock to Louis XV for £1,500 and a mechanical organ for £300 to the Grand Mogul.

Although celebrated as a maker of complicated musical clockwork for forty years, it is a curious fact that to most people Christopher Pinchbeck's name is associated only with a gold-like metal alloy evolved during the last six years of his life. Pinchbeck, real pinchbeck, has such a lovely hue that it is time collectors understood it more fully. He had found, like other clockmakers, that even the finest of English brass was untrustworthy for clock movements. It was pitted by too many microscopic air bubbles buried in the body of the metal. Cogs were weakened by such flaws and tended to crack after little use. He, like other clockmakers, used plates of latten, that is, brass sheets made absolutely solid by long beating with a water-operated battery hammer. This entailed laborious and costly handwork to bring each unit to its final clockwork precision.

During his early years in Fleet Street, Pinchbeck experimented to improve the copper-zinc alloy known as prince's metal, named after Prince Rupert, who was claimed by Daniel Defoe to be its inventor. This metal was defined in 1705 as five parts copper and one part zinc converted into an alloy by direct fusion.

Francis Hauksbee, FRS, a celebrated metallurgist with laboratories only two minutes' walk from Pinchbeck's workshop, succeeded in extracting sulphur fumes from copper, thus producing a highly purified metal known as rose copper. This meant that for the first time unpitted brass castings were possible in England from the late 1720s. Pinchbeck carried the improvement further: instead of incorporating into his alloy English zinc, then containing calamine, he used tutenag imported from China, much of it forming a protective lining to chests of tea. Tutenag was actually pure zinc, a metal then impossible to produce in England. Fused in small crucibles in the proportion of five of rose copper to one of tutenag, these methods produced an unpitted alloy capable of being cast in clear-cut relief.

Pinchbeck's next step was to colour this alloy to match

contemporaneous 22-carat gold, then recognised by the Goldsmiths' Company as the standard quality hallmark for jewellery. This he achieved by processing the cast metal, first by heating until slightly red, then, when cold, pickling it in vitriol. Dust and scale were removed by washing in water and the piece momentarily immersed in aquafortis. Decorative relief work and soft, rounded edges were clearly defined by chasing and then finally burnished with a bloodstone fluxed with oil and whiting.

The new metal was marketed as pinchbeck before 1727. A new trade card designed and engraved in that year illustrated his shop sign, now *Pinchbeck's Head*, displaying a copy of his portrait painted by Isaac Whood and engraved in mezzotint by John Faber. Simultaneously he issued an advertising token, a bust of George II on the obverse, and the reverse with a portrait of Pinchbeck himself surrounded by objects made in his workshops—a snuff-box, a cane knob, a watch attached to a double chain and a signet ring. This was inscribed around the edge: 'Christopher Pinchbeck Senior, at Pinchbeck's Head in Fleet Street.'

The metal pinchbeck achieved, quite wrongly, the reputation of being untarnishable and retaining its lustre indefinitely. True, oxidisation was a slow process, but objects made by the Pinchbeck family, cast in the solid metal, were such as demanded continual handling or were rubbed by the pocket lining whilst being carried.

Pinchbeck created his own fascinating range of handsomely hand-tooled bijouterie resembling gold such as snuff-boxes, etuis, chatelaines, cane knobs and other personal finery, showing a wholly different approach to the demand of an increasingly sophisticated and discriminating clan of the not-so-rich.

Snuff-boxes were advertised from the beginning as 'so nearly resembling gold that the best judges can hardly distinguish one from the other' and must have been made in tens of thousands. Remaining specimens inspected have the appearance of fine craftsmanship from a period when labour might be considered well-spent in giving to less costly substitutes the exquisite finish expected on snuff-boxes of gold.

The boxes were worked upon in exactly the same way that goldsmiths treated their fashionable jewellery in cast gold and silver. Pinchbeck was used alone in the majority of instances, the relief work being the outstanding feature of design. Shapes included oval, rectangle, octagon, cartouche and shell, duplicating fashionable patterns in gold. The box and cover were cast separately to be finished all over with flowers, foliate scrolls and shells against a matted ground, by a goldsmith using fine chisels, burins and various chasing tools. Punches and stamps were used for background work. The centre of the cover might be decorated with mythological heroes and heroines in the mood of the ancient cameo, with pictorial scenes or musical trophies within ovals. In one extensive series the cover was set with a flat colourful hardstone (see page 87) such as agate, sardonyx, mocha stone or cairngorm, bordered with a scroll and wave design. The sides were usually cast in bombé shape and panelled with fruit and flowers between arched pilasters. The base might be set all over with a hardstone matching that of the cover. The thumbpiece might be plain, serrated or enriched with a shell.

The earliest reference to Pinchbeck's name as denoting this metal was by Henry Fielding in 1734: 'the nobility and gentry run so much into Pinchbeck that he [the jeweller] has not dispos'd of two gold watches this month.' L. Cook in 1744 referred to 'gold, silver and pinchbeck snuff-boxes' and Lady Mary Wortley Montagu in 1755 wrote to the Countess of Bute concerning 'three of Pinchbek's watches'.

Christopher Pinchbeck died in 1732, too soon to know wide appreciation for his gold-coloured brass alloy. He was buried in St Dunstan's Church, a few yards from his retail shop. Nine days later the *Daily Post* announced that 'the snuff-boxes and other toys made by the late ingenious Mr Pinchbeck's curious metal . . . are now sold only by his son Mr Edward Pinchbeck'.

Imitators soon appeared offering an imperfect alloy masquerading as pinchbeck: there was then no legal protection against the use of a trade name. The counterfeit metal contained English zinc and instead of being processed was finished more cheaply with the period's far from satisfactory gilding. This prompted a further advertisement from Edward Pinchbeck in which he announced that he 'did not dispose of one grain of the curious metal which so nearly resembled gold in colour, smell and ductability to any person whatever'. Following the death of Edward in 1766 Pinchbeck's Head came under the control of his elder brother, Christopher II, long established as a maker of astronomical clocks at impressive premises in Cockspur Street. He became a personal friend of George III who appointed him his Principal Clockmaker. He was selected in 1768 to make a four-sided astronomical clock for the Queen's House. This was designed by the King and Sir William Chambers: the clock is now at Buckingham Palace. The Pinchbeck business was discontinued after Christopher's death in 1783.

### GILT BRASS

The Pinchbecks at no time manufactured the light gilded brass snuff-boxes and other jewellery such as were made in factory workshops and which passed under the name of pinchbeck for a century or more after 1780 when James Emerson of Henham, Bristol, patented a formula and process for making by direct fusion of copper and zinc a fine brass closely resembling pinchbeck. This was described as 'more malleable and more beautiful and of a colour more resembling gold than ordinary brass.' This golden metal, very much cheaper than the pinchbeck which it superseded, became widely used by the manufacturing jewellers and snuff-box makers of Birmingham and Clerkenwell, who pirated the name of the pinchbeck.

They made their snuff-boxes from Emerson's metal rolled by machinery and shaped with a hand-operated drop hammer patented in 1769 by John Pickersgill, London. A year later

John Smith of Birmingham developed the process to give not only form but clear relief ornament. Little use was made of this stamp in the snuff-box branch of the trade until the mid-1780s.

Production of gilded-brass snuff-boxes no longer depended upon handcraft and personal skill but upon a variety of brass alloys and power-driven machinery. By the mid-1790s the two units of a snuff-box, with provision for hinging and fastening, were stamped with tools made from a new steel, much harder and longer wearing than had formerly been available. This raised impressions in finer and higher relief, three operations being needed, with the metal annealed between each to prevent splitting. In addition to the die-sunk intaglio with the required decoration a 'force' was used. This fell snugly into the die but allowed just enough space for the thickness of the metal being shaped and at the same time raised ornamental detail. Low relief work needed but a single operation.

The units were then chased, polished and burnished or gilded. Two colours of gilding were now possible – yellow and orange. The yellow tinge was secured by the application of zinc-mercury before gilding in the usual way; as many as four coatings might be given. Dating of these inexpensive snuff-boxes is not determined accurately by style alone, since the fashion introduced by the goldsmith might be continued until the tools were worn. Even before 1800 snuff-box men were tending to speed up manufacture through use of the press, by building box and cover from several pressed units that could be quickly brazed together.

Early imitations of pinchbeck snuff-boxes in gilded brass may be found struck with small punch marks resembling the assay marks which were then struck on 22-carat gold. Because of the confusion between assay marks and trade marks on everyman's golden snuff-box, legislation became necessary and from 1798 it was illegal for any identifying marks to be struck on pinchbeck or gilded metal. It was stipulated, too, that in the case of gilded metal the amount of gold, single, double or treble, should be shown. At the same time 18-carat gold was required to show the figure 18 along with the lion passant hallmark.

Gilt-brass snuff-boxes from about 1815 might be decorated with engine-turning, the lid design incorporating a plain surfaced shield, scroll or rectangle upon which the owner's crest or, more usually, cypher might be inscribed. Cover and base were decorated to match. Designs may be counted by the hundred.

The early 1830s saw the beginning of a vogue for decorating gilt snuff-box lids with pictures in high relief, many of them from worn tools used by factory silversmiths. Such pictures included sporting scenes, adaptations of Dutch paintings, designs illustrative of Shakespeare and his works and buildings of national interest such as Windsor Castle, the Tower and London Bridge. Snuff-boxes might be electro-gilded from the early 1840s, a process which covered them with a film of pure gold, varying in thickness and wearing properties according to price.

### LANCASHIRE BRASS

When Philip Andreas Nemnich travelled England in 1799 he passed through the watch-making township of Prescot in South Lancashire and noted in his diary: 'Here the best watchmakers' tools are made and all parts of the movements of watches; while one workman is employed solely on the manufacture of watch springs, a second makes the cogged wheels such as the ratchet, minute and hour wheels, a third the barrels and barrel covers, a fourth the balance cocks, a fifth the hands. These pieces go to the clock and watch-making centres of Liverpool, Coventry and London where they are assembled and fitted into cases.'

These hand-made watch units by the early 1820s were meeting direct competition from France where machine tools were producing them at a fraction of the cost possible in England. These tools had been devised by Frederic Japy of Beaucourt, France, in 1776. He established a factory for making parts for watch movements in 1810 and a few years later his sons opened show-rooms and offices at 108 Rue du Temple, Paris. Instruments cut accurately the teeth of cogged wheels, drilled the watch plates and polished the finished parts. These standardised units could be assembled into a movement held between a pair of brass plates. The Japy brothers were selling more than half a million movements a year by 1840 and similar mass production had started in the United States of America. This effective rivalry had created drastic unemployment among the craftsmen of Prescot who had to seek other uses for their idle equipment and tools. Eventually they discovered a potential market for snuff-boxes in brass and copper, many of them fitted with simple but effective combination locks.

Brass and copper plate, in a gauge strong enough to prevent warping, were found long-wearing and inexpensive. But it was the ingenious keyless lock mechanism devised by a Prescot craftsman that resulted in the production of snuff-boxes that still intrigue collectors today. These ranged from table boxes to pocket size. Table snuff-boxes were particularly vulnerable to the petty pilferer, while the pocket box needed to be secure from spilling its valuable contents when constant use led to careless handling. The table snuff-box originally contained a tiny spoon for replenishing the pocket box.

The obvious development, then, was for the Prescot watch men to design many of these locks with combination controls on the lids to delight and puzzle late Georgians and early Victorians. The controls resembled a pair of crudely engraved watch dials numbered from one to twelve and fitted with circling pointers. By setting the pointers to certain pre-arranged numbers the box's catch-fastener could be released. In some instances there was also a third control pointer in the shape of a sun in splendour. The catch for opening the box might be in the shape of the first or last quarter of the moon: this slid back to open the lid and forward to latch it when closed. All joints were soldered to prevent seepage and the surfaces of the solder wiped smooth.

The locking mechanism was attached to the underside of the lid and protected from clogging by a covering plate of brass or iron. This was sealed at the edges with solder made from equal quantities of brass and zinc, to prevent snuff from seeping through the joints. The interior was heavily tinned to prevent the snuff from acquiring a metallic tang.

In many instances a five-lug hinge extended the full width of the pocket snuff-box, securely riveted with brass wire. Constant opening and shutting tended to wear the lugs of the hinge, causing the lid to fit loosely and allow snuff to leak into the pocket.

Shuttle-shaped pocket snuff-boxes such as were fashionable during the fourth quarter of the 18th century achieved renewed popularity in brass and copper. The example illustrated (No. 15 between pages 64–65) is in copper decorated with ornament resembling the bright-cut engraving used on silver plate, wriggled and punched work with an engraved monogram and, around the sides, the inscription *May the Wings of Liberty Never want a Feather*. This suggests that the owner was a supporter of the Reform Bill and that this box was made during the early 1830s. The lid is fitted with a pair of revolving studs: these are marked with short arrows which, when correctly placed, secure or release the catch.

The majority of these snuff-boxes were sold plain, either of brass highly burnished or of an alloy more closely resembling the colour of gold. Others were decorated with simple chasing or punched and wriggled work, or were line engraved with motifs such as sporting and maritime scenes, flowers and foliage, scrollwork and inscriptions. The owner's name or initials and date were frequently introduced. *Memento mori* snuff-boxes in this style may be found. Typically the box was engraved with the deceased's name and date of death accompanied by a suitable text or inscription and an 'all-seeing eye'. Frequently the inscription indicates that the snuff-box was carried by a mourner in lieu of the more usual finger ring.

Coffin-shaped snuff-boxes inscribed with allusions to death

were common. A specimen with a combination lock to its brass
lid may be found with sides and base appropriately made from
a hollowed-out block of box wood, the lugubrious tone of the
piece being completed by an inscription such as *Sacred to the
Dust of A.B.*

An interesting series of pocket snuff-boxes intended for the
thrifty have a somewhat simpler and less fool-proof form of
opening which avoided the use of a hinge. The box sides consisted of a circular, oval, square, hexagonal or octagonal ring of
close-grained hardwood such as box wood or lignum vitae,
usually stained dark red. This wooden ring was sandwiched
between a pair of brass plates riveted or screwed into the wood.
The bottom plate was solid but the upper plate was cut with a
figure 8 opening and over this was superimposed a second plate
similarly pierced and revolving on a central pivot. Such a box
was opened by revolving the top plate by means of a stud fitted
for that purpose, until the two openings coincided. The finger
and thumb were then inserted through the suitably shaped
aperture. No more than the smallest of 'pinches' could be taken
owing to the inability of the snuffer to separate finger and
thumb. The bottom plate might be engraved with an inscription or name and the rim of the static plate beyond the edge of
the revolving cover might be decorated with wriggled work or
conventional suns in splendour. Engraving filling the area of
the static plate revealed when the revolving lid was fully closed
served as an aid to the careful snuffer. This simple style of
opening may be found, too, on a snuff-box shaped as a brass-
bound book.

The table snuff-box with a lift-off lid was typical of Prescot
design and craftsmanship. It is in heavy copper plate with its
combination lock controlled by three domed dials. These are
engraved with the rising sun, the sun in splendour and the
setting sun with a crescent moon to operate the catch. Its
Prescot origin is confirmed by the rim encircled with hour
numerals and divisions resembling a clock dial. The centre is
engraved with twelve petals in outline.

A popular type of table snuff-box was hammered into the shape of a large watch case with boldly curved sides and convex lid measuring $3\frac{1}{2}$ to 4 in. across and nearly 2 in. deep, often fitted with a circular bow above the hinge for hanging perhaps in office or workshop.

In some instances a number will be found stamped beneath such a snuff-box. Since these range from the 1500s to the 1900s they are often mistaken for dates of manufacture. But in fact such a number is no more than the craftsman's way of numbering each box he made consecutively in the manner he had used in better days to mark his watches. When a metal ring swings from a small eye riveted beneath the hinge or elsewhere, the snuff-box dates later than the introduction of the double albert in the late 1840s.

Snuff-boxes with combination locks have been reproduced in the present century. They may be recognised by their construction from light-weight rolled brass of more golden hue than the originals.

Many early Victorian snuff-boxes in these designs were made at Wolverhampton, which for more than a century had been the centre of the brass tobacco and snuff-box trade. These were mostly exported to the continent and many are now returning to collectors as Dutch antiques. Self-acting spring snuff-boxes in gilt brass were shown at the Great Exhibition of 1851.

1   Colley Cibber (1671–1757), celebrated actor and dramatist, poet laureate
from 1730, taking a pinch of snuff from a tortoiseshell snuff-box shaped as a
scallop shell. Mezzotint engraving by Jean Simon (1675–1751) after the
painting by Giuseppe Grisoni (1699–1769).
In the British Museum.

2   Sheffield plate table snuff-rasp. Two-thirds of the canoe-shaped container is covered with a hinged grater: the remainder supports a box large enough to carry a small carotte for grating.
In the Sheffield City Museum.

3   Pocket snuff-rasp cases of carved wood. In each example the cover swivels on a joint at the wide end to expose the perforated grater fixed over a shallow recess. The snuff was removed through a grooved channel cut in the narrow end.
In the Victoria and Albert Museum.

Or since the Parish Clerk said Amen. · Or in a Twelvemonth and a Day. · But continued true and in defire.
·ished yourfelves Unmarried again. · Repented not in thought any way. · As when you joined hands in holy quire.

*The Proceffion after claiming the Gammon of Bacon at the Monaftry of great Dunmow in Essex.*
W. Sherwin Sculp!

4   Snuff-handkerchief printed with 'The Procession after claiming the Gammon of Bacon at the Monastery of Great Dunmow in Essex'. Engraved by William Sherwin in the 1780s.
In the Victoria and Albert Museum.

5   Table snuff-boxes of papier-mâché with rimmed lids, each signed 'S. Raven Pinxt. Patronized by H.R.H. the Duke of Sussex and Prince Leopold'. (*Left to right*) Mary, Queen of Scots; Miss Foote, the actress; the Three Graces. Late 1820s.

6 Silver snuff-box set with a medal of Clementina Sobieski, wife of the Old Pretender, struck in 1719. The border engraved with formal design. Shell and scroll thumbpiece. About 1750.
Christies.

7 Ivory table snuff-box with lift-off cover set with a portrait of George IV carved in relief. Diameter $3\frac{1}{2}$ in.
In the Victoria and Albert Museum.

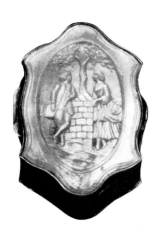

8 (*Above left*) Gold shell-shaped snuff-box, the cover chased with putti playing with doves before a classical colonnade. Interior of the cover inset with a miniature portrait by Gervaise Spencer, signed and dated 1749. 2½ in. long.
Christies.

9 (*Above right*) Gold snuff-box engine-turned, the borders chased with bands of green-gold foliage. By Jacob Amedroz, 1799.
Christies.

10 (*Centre left*) Mother of pearl, carved in low relief, set in a silver box. Late 18th century.
Christies.

11 (*Bottom left*) Gold snuff-box, with slightly bombé sides, the cover set with a plaque of painted enamel. The sides chased with flowers, feathers and scrolls. George II period. 1⅞ in. diameter.
Christies.

12 (*Bottom right*) Gold mounted snuff-box set with café au lait agate panels. 2 in. diameter.
Christies.

13    Sheffield plate snuff-boxes constructed of copper plated with silver on one side only. The sides are seamed, invisible outside; the covers hand-chased and the bases decorated with die-stamped patterns. Box and cover are lined with tortoiseshell to prevent snuff from clogging in indentations. The example on the right is pierced and set with aventurine. 1750s.
In the Sheffield City Museum.

14    Rectangular snuff-box of sturdy Sheffield plate, set with a copper half-penny of the third issue of George III, struck by Matthew Boulton in 1799. The coin has been close-plated with silver which has proved far more susceptible to wear than the plate box. About 1800.
In the collection of Mrs V. S. Mitcheson.

15   Lancashire shuttle-shaped pocket snuff-box in copper decorated with bright-cut engraving and owner's initials.

16   Lancashire watch-shaped table snuff-box in brass with combination lock operated by a pair of pointers and a sun in splendour.

17 Table snuff-box in yellow Staffordshire enamel, the cover brightly coloured over a transfer print of 'The Corner Game'. Flowers in full colours decorate the sides.
In the collection of H.M. the Queen.

18 Snuff-boxes in Staffordshire enamel. The top box has an inner lid of gilt metal with a loop for holding a snuff-spoon. The double box has two lids hinged at the centre and a gilt central partition. The box on the right is painted with a portrait of William Pitt, Earl of Chatham.
In the collection of H.M. the Queen.

19 Silver-gilt snuff-box, the centre of the cover set with the Sancroft medal 1688 within a border of scrolls, flowers and wave ornament with waisted sides and plain scroll thumb-piece. 1730s. 2¾ in. diameter. Christies.

20 Table snuff-box in 18-carat gold, the chiselled scroll and floral work framing a miniature painted by Andrew Plimer. By A. J. Strachan, 1808. Asprey & Co.

21    Table snuff-box in silver-gilt, the cover engraved with two figures amid fruit, vines and scrolling foliage, the borders chased in high relief with flowers and foliage and the sides and base engine-turned. By Nathaniel Mills, Birmingham, 1827.
Christies.

22    Musical snuff-box with humming bird: early 19th century.
In the collection of H.M. the Queen.

23 (*Left*) Amethyst box of compressed spherical form, the centre of the cover with an applied gold plaque. 2⅛ in. diameter. Mid-18th century.
(*Right*) Gold-mounted agate, the border chased and pierced with flowers and scrolls. 1⅝ in. diameter. About 1760.
Christies.

24 Shell-shaped gold snuff-boxes, covers inset with amber coloured agate plaques. (*Above*) Borders and sides engraved with birds, fruits, musical trophies and foliage. Width 2⅞ in. About 1730. (*Below*) Concave sides chased with fluting and wave motifs on a matted ground. Width 3¼ in. About 1740. Christies.

25  Gold mounted snuff-box, the cover and base of mocha agate, the sides engraved with festoons of flowers and foliage on a hatched ground between key pattern borders. By Elias Russel, London, 1768. 2¾ in.
Christies.

26  Set with panels of translucent and mottled grey and brown agate, overlaid with chased cartouches of gold cage-work. About 1770.
Christies.

27   Table snuff-mull made from a ram's horn with silver snuff-box and fittings.
Height 8 in. About 1820.
In the Victoria and Albert Museum.

28 Pontypool japanned snuff-boxes, all with pull-off covers. Mid-18th century. In the National Museum of Wales.

29 Clouté d'or or nailhead piqué on ivory. The hand-worked facets are
virtually touching. About 1800.

30 Table snuff-box in Sheffield plate with pull-off cover of tortoiseshell
ornamented in silver posé piqué. Made in about 1750 by Thomas Bolsover,
the inventor of Sheffield plate.
In the collection of Mrs V. S. Mitcheson.

31  Double snuff-box of agate with gold mounts hinged centrally and chased with scrolls, flowers and wave ornament, the sides with eight pilasters. About 1740.
Christies.

32  Double table snuff-box in silver, one of a pair. By John Edwards, London, 1802. Length $4\frac{3}{4}$ in.
Prestons Ltd.

CHAPTER 6

# Painted Enamels

ONE OF the most delightful manufactures of Georgian artist-craftsmen was the snuff-box in painted enamel. These are as brilliantly colourful today as when they left the workshop bench. Essentially this wholly English craft met the needs of innumerable men and women who adored elegant little trifles to match their studied graces but could never afford the exclusive creations of goldsmiths and jewellers. They delighted in tiny enamelled boxes for snuff or breath-sweetening comfits or fragments of sponge soaked in aromatic vinegar.

It has been established that some of these trifles were made at Bilston in Staffordshire as early as the late 1740s and the craft continued unceasingly for about a century, snuff-boxes being produced in their hundreds of thousands. In contrast, the Battersea factory that has given these enamels their most popular collector-name lasted no longer than three years, 1753–56.

Painted enamels were produced by fusing what amounted to opacified flint-glass to the surface of paper-thin copper and adding coloured decoration by brush, often over transfer-printed outlines, lasting brilliance being given by firing in a muffle kiln. Edges were rimmed with metal neatly hand-tooled and gilded: assembly was so perfect that none of these snuff-boxes ever required a fastener.

The Battersea factory established by Stephen Theodore Janssen at York House, former London residence of the Arch-bishops of York, no doubt materialised because the sponsors were confident of the commercial advantages of decorating enamels with transferred prints, a process evolved at Battersea.

The basic white enamel used at Battersea was probably entirely hand-prepared. Soft, in several tones of creamy white with

5

65

warm, brilliant surface qualities, this enamel proved an excellent ground for hand-painted decoration carried out in full but not heavy colour with fusible pigments. Colours melted over it with delightful translucent effect, and transfer prints copied excellently. The high glaze on Battersea snuff-boxes suggests that lead oxide played an important part in its composition.

The colours found in Battersea monochrome transfer printing were mauve, near-black, crimson and brick red. The copper plates were cut with deep incisions sunk in such a way that they held the enamel oil-ink firmly, yet permitted printing on paper with clear-cut, even lines when plate and ink were warmed to an equal temperature. Considerable additions were sometimes made by the enamel painter: in others there is evidence of touching up with pencil brush work in a matching shade. But the majority required no such subsequent tinting.

Stylistically their treatment mainly reflected cultivated French taste of the mid-18th century. Their decoration was dominated by the wholly graceful, slightly effeminate engravings of Simon-François Ravenet who is prominent in Battersea work. He and his fellows catered for a sophisticated enjoyment of daintily illustrated classical lore, and a knowledgeable appreciation of high-quality single-colour printing over lustrous enamel. Artists painted as thinly as possible as thick applications tended to split during cooling after firing: the labour cost of preparing the coloured enamels was high. On Battersea snuff-boxes the decoration usually covered the whole surface of the lid, without the gilding characteristic of subsequent South Staffordshire work.

For their subjects the engravers most frequently turned to the popular prints of the period. Portraits of royalty and other celebrities were executed with masterly precision on snuff-boxes: the reverse of a lid might be decorated with another print, its subject not necessarily associated with that on the outer surface. On the sides of the box, and perhaps on the base too, might appear painted flowers or such recurrent printed motifs as Ravenet's cupid groups and representations of the arts.

Among the few known decorators at Battersea were the Irishmen John Brooks, first to apply the idea of copper-plate printing to industrial purposes, and James Gwin who, John Williams has stated, arrived in London in 1755 when he 'got his livelihood by making designs for the lids of snuff-boxes, which he did for a manufactory at Battersea under the direction of Sir Stephen Janssen.' But the most important associate in the venture was Robert Hancock, himself an engraver of copper plates who is credited with introducing transfer-printing to the ceramics industry.

The final stage in the production of a Battersea snuff-box was the fitting of the hinged mount to rim and lid. The enamel, applied to both faces of the thin copper with a spatula, could not be made to adhere to the sharp edges of the copper. This problem was solved by binding all exposed edges in thin frames of copper or copper alloy. In the announcement of the sale at York House, Battersea, there is reference to 'copper frames for mounting the enamels' but in the list of enamels sold from Janssen's City home the description of the snuff-boxes includes 'mostly mounted in metal, double-gilt'.

After the closure of the Battersea factory early in 1756 the *Daily Advertiser* announced that a sale of Janssen's household effects included 'a quantity of beautiful enamels, colour'd and uncolour'd . . . consisting of Snuff-boxes of all sizes and in a great variety of Patterns'. The sale of the stock-in-trade at York House also included 'a great variety of beautiful enamell'd snuff-boxes'. Painted enamels still continued to be made in London. In 1760 J. Morris of Norris Street, Haymarket, advertised that he 'Manufactured all sorts of Enamel'd Work in Snuff Boxes'.

Painted enamels pre-dating the Battersea productions were made by John Taylor, a Birmingham button maker who in 1755 employed some 500 persons. Taylor, no doubt the pioneer in the manufacture of cheap enamelled snuff-boxes and the like, was probably established in the trade before 1750. Not only was he fully equipped with the basic facilities for making the copper blanks and mounts, but he was also a partner in a flint-glass works at Stourbridge.

William Hutton, a contemporary of Taylor and well-known to him, in his *History of Birmingham* published in 1781, wrote: 'To this uncommon genius we owe the gilt button, the japanned [?] and gilt snuff-boxes, with the numerous race of enamels. From the same fountain issued the painted snuff-box, at which one servant earned £3 10 0 by painting them at a farthing each.' If such a painter worked a six-day week and the 14-hour day of the period, this rate of production approximated 30 boxes an hour. Obviously this suggests that he must have employed an assistant, but even with such help his work at the best must have been extremely crude. The basic enamel on these snuff-boxes was applied by spatula. It is probable that speedy production and incomplete understanding of the processes involved resulted in snuff-boxes from which the enamel soon flaked and chipped off the copper base so that few are encountered by collectors.

Taylor himself was a successful man of business, unlikely to take up an enterprise which did not promise profitable results, as may be gathered by the comment of James Watt in a letter to Matthew Boulton in 1775: 'John Taylor died the other day worth £200,000 without ever doing one generous action.'

Taylor was by no means the only Birmingham enameller. Basil Palmer is recorded in the 1767 *Directory* as an enameller and button-maker. The craft continued unceasingly in Birmingham until the 1840s. *Robson's Directory*, 1839, lists three enamellers: Charles Gwynne, 16 Mott Street; J. Abrahall, 4 Caroline Street; and John Brown & Co., 69 Bull Street.

Matthew Boulton, trading as Boulton & Fothergill, is usually referred to as of Birmingham, but actually was at Soho in South Staffordshire. His trade card of the 1770s illustrated his premises. Confirmation of enamel manufacture is plentiful and includes a reference in a letter written to James Adam in 1770. Queen Mary possessed a double snuff-box by Boulton with a gilded silver mount struck with the hall-mark for 1783.

For some years prior to the establishment of Janssen's

Battersea factory, South Staffordshire and Birmingham were the most important producers of enamel snuff-boxes. Early collectors established the fame of the Battersea work, but only recently has there been a long over-due evaluation of South Staffordshire enamels.

The craft of japanning on iron had been established in Bilston as early as the reign of Queen Anne and it has now been confirmed that a group of enamellers from France arrived in this town some time before 1745 and taught the local japanners what was hailed at the time as an improved art of decorating. Contemporaneously, and throughout the first half of the 18th century, the Bilston parish registers refer to a number of snuff-box makers.

Here in Bilston, with the flint-glass centre of Stourbridge only a few miles away to the south-west, was an obvious centre for anyone wishing to produce decorative enamels on a commercial scale and requiring rolled copper, metal mounts, enamel colours and decorators. With reasonable certainty the 1740s have been credited with the circular snuff-boxes of japanned iron with detachable lids inset with painted enamel plaques.

The earliest industrial enameller of whom any personal record exists was Dovey Hawkesford of Bilston. He was described in 1741 as a chapman, but at the time of his death in 1749 the news columns of *Aris's Birmingham Gazette* reported him as having been an enameller. This is confirmed by the fact that at this time Benjamin Bickley bought a fully equipped enamel factory in Bilston, advertised as possessing 'a pair of millstones and two mills for grinding enamels.' This was almost five years before the Battersea venture was launched.

From the examples that remain today it is clear that the main development of Bilston enamelling dates from about 1750. At once it is necessary to reject the old idea of one or two individual enamellers whose hand may be detected in all the major South Staffordshire productions. It has been established that more than eighteen master enamellers operated at Bilston. These included the Bickley, Perry and Becket families, James Brett,

John Buckley, J. Hoo Foster, John Green, S. Hanson, Thomas Knowles and Isaac Smith. Local directory records tell their own tale of the rise and fall of the trade.

Enamelling was established at near-by Wednesbury in 1776 by Samuel Yardley who obtained the necessary equipment from the sale of the Bickley factory in that year. It has not been fully appreciated that this marked a distinctive new phase in the development of enamelling. Yardley found that costs could be cut drastically by dipping the shaped copper into thick liquid enamel. At the same time enamelling furnaces became more efficient and were enlarged. By 1780 other enamellers were established in Wednesbury, all using the dipping process and improved furnaces to the detriment of the Bilston enamellers who continued applying the viscid paste to the copper by means of spatulas. Soon a second coating of fine quality enamel might be applied over the basic layer: the two qualities are visible in cracks.

The men associated with the manufacture of Wednesbury enamels include three generations of Yardleys, the families of Holden, Ross, Baker and Snape. There are several contemporaneous references to the excellence of their work. It was James Ross who evolved the formula for the delicate pink tinted enamel and for many years he was the sole maker. Many of these enamellers made snuff-boxes, in some cases sending them out to independent decorators for painting or transfer printing, receiving them back, already muffle-fired, for mounting and finishing. At the same time several mount-makers bought decorated lids of good quality from one supplier and second quality bodies from another source, fitted them together and sold them to merchants at competitive prices. Snuff-boxes are often found with the basic white enamels on body and lid of obviously different qualities.

Snuff-boxes in what is sometimes described as the Battersea style usually have their lids enriched with pictorial decoration and the sides with additional pictures or hand-painted posies. Some elaborately mounted snuff-boxes are brightly but somewhat laboriously painted with subjects adapted from engravings such as that by De Larmessin of Lancret's 'L'après-dîner'. These constitute a distinctive group preceding the more mechanical style of painting associated with factory productions. Colours are usually bright with particular emphasis on yellows and reds over red-brown printed outlines.

At this period the most highly decorative style of picture was largely the province of French artists and it is scarcely surprising to find the works of Watteau, Lancret, Boucher and Nattier copied on snuff-boxes. For instance, a rectangular snuff-box lid might display one or other of Antoine Watteau's gay scenes such as his *Fêtes Venitiennes* or *Le Colin Maillard*. Other frequently copied works are Nicolas Lancret's *Flute Lesson* and *Tea Party* (the latter in many extremely fine adaptations), *Les Amants* by Jean-Marc Nattier and *Pensent-ils au Raisins?* by François Boucher.

Among the mezzotint engravers whose work was adapted by the South Staffordshire enamellers may be mentioned Richard Houston who popularised Philippe Mercier's series *Morning*, *Afternoon* and so on: the vivacious study of a woman holding a mask from *Night* in this series is frequently encountered on snuff-box lids. François Vivares produced several engravings of classical landscapes by Claude Lorraine and others which, more or less standardised, appeared on innumerable painted enamels.

The classical landscapes decorating South Staffordshire enamel boxes are pleasantly drawn and carefully coloured, but they are unambitious routine pieces of work in line with the contemporary demand for pillared ruins and pastoral scenes. Only very occasionally do people and animals come to life.

Not until the 1760s were enamelled snuff-boxes given gilded decoration, which could not be burnished to a rich lustre and lacks the brilliance of later gilding. Even when new this gold was slightly dull in appearance and would not withstand wear. South Staffordshire gilding from the 1780s involved the use of mercury and was a serious health hazard.

During the period of South Staffordshire's finest production, the 1760s to the early 1780s, a painted enamel snuff-box might be a truly handsome possession. The outer surfaces of box and lid were smooth and flawless. Superimposed upon this background, which might be tinted in such colours as blue, green or pink, there might be a raised diaper pattern of criss-cross lines interspersed with dots, all in white or one or more harmonising colours.

The slightly convex lid of the typical snuff-box was decorated with elaborate scrollwork applied in raised white enamel covered with gilding; sometimes this might embody tiny flower posies painted in full colour on white reserves among the scroll-work. The central white reserve of the lid, within the irregularly shaped rococo scrolling, was painted in full colour with or without the basis of a transfer print, and on each side of the box a white reserve among more gilded scrolls contained another tiny picture painted in full colour – often by a different hand on the finest snuff-boxes – or a simple flower posy. In some examples the base carried another posy in colour or a single flower in gilt. A peculiarly straggly gilt flower is probably the trade symbol of an individual firm and other symbols which may eventually be identified include central dot-and-dash designs on raised white, applied like the diaper work covering the rest of the box.

Slight embossing on enamel snuff-boxes dates from the late 1760s: a box decorated in this way has been noted with an inscription dated 1769. By 1775 deep press-embossing had become fashionable, such as is seen in the snuff-box with a rose embossed on the lid, each petal painted in detail. (Some of these closely resembled Meissen porcelain).

Until the French Revolution the majority of Staffordshire enamels went abroad, principally to France and Italy. With these markets lost, the final phase of these delightful snuff-boxes was dominated by the need to cut costs. By the 1790s quality was being sacrificed disastrously and the market flooded with innumerable tiny snuff-boxes in no way comparable with the early issues. The collector must look beyond these intriguing but unambitious trifles if he is to appreciate the English painted enamels' colourful contribution to 18th-century manufactures.

Typical of the late mass production work were the little boxes in dullish colours, usually oval, less well-hinged and lacking applied base rims, which nevertheless were so well constructed that they never required fasteners to secure their contents of snuff. Even at the time these were regarded largely as souvenirs to be sold or presented by shop-keepers at fashionable watering places and holiday resorts. Many were printed with local views and the inscription *A Trifle from* – Tunbridge Wells, Cheltenham, Bath, Harrogate, Evesham, Worcester, Stafford, Stone, even Wolverhampton, to name only a few towns. Some bore, in addition, painted in, the name of the shops that presented them to favoured customers.

A small snuff-box, transfer-printed and hand-coloured with a portrait of Queen Caroline, was issued early in the reign of George IV (probably in 1821) when according to *Parson and Bradshaw's Directory*, 1820, only two South Staffordshire enamellers were operating: Isaac Becket, Duck Lane, Bilston, and John Yardley, Church Hill, Wednesbury, both entered as enamel box makers.

Early snuff-box mounts are notable for their superb craftsmanship. They were fitted to the edges of the enamelled body and lid and known to the trade as 'jointed mounts'. Specialist mount-makers in Bilston served the painted enamel trade and there were several in Wolverhampton and Birmingham. Decoration on the earliest mounts, made from thin ribbons of pinchbeck, was restricted to short tooled lines and punchings such as the craftsman's time and ingenuity allowed. The first technial improvement came in 1768 with the introduction of the steel swage block through which a ribbon of soft brass could be drawn so that its cross section could be of any desired ornamental shape. These swage-shaped ribbons were too flimsy to be used alone as mounts and were therefore hard soldered to slightly heavier plain ribbons which were fabricated into hinged mounts. Such built-up mounts are distinctive and are associated with enamels made before the era of cut-price production. Edge decoration on this ribbon was still hand-worked with such simple motifs as beading and gadrooning. The inevitable irregularities of handwork distinguish it from machine-made patterns. These date from 1779 onward when William Bell patented a process for decorating the outer surface of profiled ribbons by means of 'rolling cylinders, the cylinder being shaped to suit the design. These are of great benefit to the toy trade'.

Hinges were usually four-jointed, but in the case of rectangular and square boxes they extended the full width of the box. Hinges on inexpensive souvenir snuff-boxes had three joints. Most hinges were carefully made to withstand the severe wear of a snuff-box being continually opened and shut. From about 1790 a slight deterioration in craftsmanship may be noted. A shapely lifter or thumb-piece was fitted to the front edge of the lid.

Careful examination of suspected London reproductions reveals the marks of press tools around the hinges, some of which have a small central projection. But reproductions made by Samson & Co., Paris, do not have this defect.

# CHAPTER 7

# Musical Boxes: Singing Birds

## MUSICAL BOXES

GEORGIAN elegance found expression in many a tiny snuff-box exquisitely enriched with embossments and jewels. But even more splendid was the snuff-box which, with slight pressure upon a concealed button, chimed and tinkled a melodious accompaniment to an invitation to participate in the ceremony of snuffing. Such boxes provided precisely the quality of surprise that fascinated and delighted rich Georgians.

Musical snuff-boxes in England date from the early 1770s to the 1860s and are usually cased in hallmarked silver or silver-gilt: rarely in gold before the mid-1850s. Queen Mary possessed several that had formerly belonged to Queen Charlotte in which the aroma of Georgian snuff still lingered.

Shapes, sizes and decorations resembled those of fashionable pocket snuff-boxes, but many were designed for the table. Early examples were of plainly polished silver, followed by chasing. During the 1780s and early 1790s there was a fashion for bright-cut engraving, followed by cast and chased decoration from 1800, and, in the early 19th century, by engine-turning. From about 1820 the cover design usually incorporated a cartouche for the attachment of a cast and chased coat of arms or crest.

The majority of early cases were hallmarked in London: on those made between 1790 and the mid-19th century Birmingham hallmarks are common and some of Glasgow.

In the 18th century the cover opened directly to the snuff compartment. The musical movement beneath was separated by a plate of semi-transparent polished horn through which the mechanism was visible. This was always sealed. The flat base

75

was hinged and highly polished. From about 1800 the positions were reversed, the cover opening to the musical movement with the snuff-box beneath. Dimensions approximated 3 in. by 2 in. by 1 in., the silver case weighing about 5½ oz and the movement about 2½ oz extra. The movement, the work of a skilled watchmaker, covered the entire area of the case and was about ¼ in. deep. At first only a single tune could be played but the number was gradually increased until by the 1830s as many as six tunes could be played within the confines of a small snuff-box.

Until about 1815 movements were simple, a 1¼ in. brass disc set with twenty steel striking pins radiating fan-wise from a central point on each side. These plucked a resonant metal comb cut with fifteen to twenty-five teeth tuned to scale. By about 1810 mechanism began to be improved and the disc was superseded by a revolving cylinder of brass from which steel pins projected. Cylinder and comb were placed parallel and provided with a spring to wind and thus operate the automatic music.

Specialists in Geneva, such as comb-makers, cylinder prickers and spring-makers supplied parts for the movements. In London the makers and assemblers of movements often worked as garret masters. Benson & Hill, London, were spring-makers late in the 18th century whose signed work is sometimes discovered. Complete movements were imported from Switzerland and Germany throughout the period by agents in Clerkenwell and Birmingham who fitted them into boxes made by English jewellers.

Less expensive musical snuff-boxes were made from about 1815 with outer cases of jet black horn. Covers were often decorated with impressed views, classical scenes, oval portraits of celebrities, or sometimes scrollwork enriched with gilding long since worn away. Engine-turned decoration was also used. These sold in large numbers for more than half a century.

Wood snuff-box cases became popular from the mid-1820s, such as maple, palm-tree, olive wood, amboyna, coromandel, rosewood, fruit woods, with covers attractively grained: lignum vitae was also used. In one popular series the cover was inlaid with a design composed of trumpet, tambourine, music sheet and other musical trophies accompanied by an olive branch.

A musical snuff-box typical of a series recorded in the *Penny Magazine for the Society for Diffusion of Useful Knowledge*, 1838, 'usually plays two tunes repeatedly, the pins being fixed and immovable. However, pins could be fixed to play almost any tune desired: usually they come in fancy boxes with the mechanism visible under a sheet of horn. Some of the larger snuff-boxes can play as many as six different tunes.' A cheap musical snuff-box sold the world over from 1835 was operated by a worm screw and had neither spring nor speed regulator. The boxes were of japanned iron hand-painted in colours or, from about 1860, decorated with coloured transfers. These snuff-boxes played but a single tune and were also counted as interesting toys for children.

Popular tunes were used almost exclusively until the 1830s, often selections from operas. Waltzes were in continual demand from the 1830s together with ballads and patriotic and folk songs until about 1850. Airs from oratorios date from about 1845. Musical snuff-boxes inspired at least two musical compositions: *The Snuff-Box Waltz* by M.S. in 1830 and *The Musical Snuff-Box* by Anatul Liadov.

Musical snuff-boxes may be dated by the style of the case, the type of ornament used, the progressive improvement in the mechanism and the selection of tunes. For instance, the positions of the steel pins, until about the middle of the century, were marked off by hand and holes bored into which they were fitted. This was a tedious process, costly in labour, for only very skilful craftsmen with a thoroughly accurate musical ear could be employed. Every cylinder was separately marked and careful inspection will reveal the scriber lines. Hollow punches ensured that the pins were accurately and firmly positioned. Warm sealing composition was then run into the cylinder and its ends covered with brass.

During the period 1810–60 amber-coloured tortoiseshell musical snuff-boxes were made with gold or silver mounts and embossed medallions set in their covers. At first these were imported from Jacquard Brothers, St Croix. These progressively played two, three, four and, by the early 1830s, six tunes. Thereafter they were made in Birmingham by William Hall, Newhall Street and Heeley Harris & Co., Lemon Street, both of whom imported Swiss movements. The name of the maker might be scratched microscopically beneath the brass plate of the mechanism, such as A. Bordier, Geneva, on a series of exceptionally fine musical snuff-boxes made from about 1785; C. Friderico, Geneva, a specialist in small watches who supplied mechanisms for musical snuff-boxes from about 1800 to 1820; and C. Brugercia, London, 1820–24. J. H. Heller, Berne, supplied good quality mechanisms from 1870 to the 1890s. The winding key was usually concealed in a tiny compartment in the bottom of the box, invisible because covered with a slide matching the case. Music was produced on opening the lid.

Musical snuff-boxes for the table contained larger movements than the pocket variety. The majority were in black horn or papier mâché and early examples even play two tunes. A depression in the dividing horn near the fastener and extending the whole width of the box accommodated a snuff-ladle.

### SINGING BIRDS

A particular treasure among a collector's snuff-boxes is the specimen with a hidden spring in the side which if lightly touched opens a trap door in the cover releasing a brilliantly plumaged bird that turns and flutters in an ecstasy of trilling song and then as suddenly disappears again. Such boxes were made in materials ranging from plain blonde tortoiseshell to jewelled and chased gold. No technique at the jeweller's disposal which added to their splendour was considered too costly.

The trap-door which released the tiny bird, seldom exceeding $\frac{3}{4}$ in. overall, was fitted into the centre of the snuff-box lid and was usually enriched with a colourful picture in enamels such as a portrait, posy or coat of arms. This panel was encircled with pearls, diamonds or other precious stones. The melodious song was accomplished by applying the basic principle that a whistling note could be created by air pressure, first demonstrated in 300 BC by the engineer Philo of Byzantium. This was applied to singing bird boxes in the late-1760s and to snuffboxes in about 1790, a whole range of notes being produced with a series of flutes similar to those on a pipe organ, but other integral parts were crude. Ten years elapsed before virtual perfection of mechanism was attained.

These delicate creations are found in a variety of detail, but there is no variation in the mechanical principle. The bird song is generated by forcing air, by means of tiny bellows, into a tube with a whistle outlet. In this tube operates a piston, its motion controlled by cam wheels. These movements modify and vary the tone and volume of the whistle sound. Motive power is provided by a coiled spring, the speed at which it uncoils being regulated by a governing mechanism.

The tiny bellows, less than one-inch square, is constructed on a copper wire frame covered with fine skin of the chicken-skin variety, so prepared that it is air-tight as well as exceptionally supple. When the spring operates the bellows air is forced through the piston tube. This produces a single long-drawn note which the intricately designed mechanism converts into the characteristic extensive tone range.

The tiny bird itself contains further mechanism causing the head to turn from side to side, beak to open and shut, wings and tail to flutter and the whole body to turn from side to side. The real master stroke was to make the bird flat so that it could be concealed in a shallow box until pressure upon a tiny lever made the cover spring open. Immediately the bird rises upright it begins to sing. At the end of the song it returns into the box and the lid snaps shut. All these automatic movements were timed to a split second. Birds of the 18th century were enamelled and not feathered, nor could they turn their heads.

In the manufacture of singing bird boxes time did not count. The making of a single example required the services of a master watch-maker to supply the mechanism; a first class jeweller and goldsmith; an artist enameller and bird-maker, additional to the assembler.

Singing bird boxes were first made in about 1770 by Peter Jacquet-Droz, a celebrated Swiss watch-maker. Eventually he reduced the mechanism to miniature proportions suitable for fitting into snuff-boxes, by replacing the series of flutes with a single piston moving backwards and forwards in a tube. This discovery was copied by the watch-makers of Geneva. It is known that before 1790 at least two dozen master-men had overcome the intricacies of manufacture and were engaged in their production until about 1830. A second series was made between 1860 and the 1930s. The earlier signed singing bird snuff-boxes were made by Jacob Frisart between 1790 and 1812: during ten of those years he worked in London. Boxes marked FR were made by Rochat et Fils, Brassus, Switzerland, founded in 1802. They moved to Geneva in 1810 and traded as Frères Rochat until 1825. These snuff-boxes imported into London repeated the elegance of early Georgian snuff-boxes ranging from specimens in 22-carat gold, chased, jewelled and enamelled to those of plain amber and tortoiseshell.

A simplified mechanism was devised in about 1860 and singing birds enhanced less expensive snuff-boxes. Their cases might be in silver-gilt, silver or gilded brass, stamped from the plate and outwardly resembling vinaigrettes or early 19th-century snuff-boxes. Those made in the 1930s sold in London at fifteen guineas each.

# CHAPTER 8

# Jasper Ware: Pottery and Porcelain

WHEN Josiah Wedgwood, FRS, in 1766 outlined his proposals for establishing a new pottery at Stoke-upon-Trent, he specified that production should include 'snuff and other boxes'. He did not market snuff-boxes, however, until he had developed the fine white stoneware that he named jasper ware, so called because its density and hardness made it possible for the lapidary's wheel to produce a polish as brilliant as that of the natural stone. It was not until 1776 that he was able to declare 'we are now absolute with jasper'.

Jasper ware is basically a vitreous semi-porcelain converted into a close-textured stoneware by the addition of barium carbonate. Its smooth non-porous surface was secured without the application of glaze and when pressed thin it revealed translucency. At first it had a creamy hue. Experiments continued and by 1780 a perfectly white jasper was made. Wedgwood's log detailing thousands of trials still remains.

Variations in the quality of jasper ware permit snuff-boxes to be dated with some accuracy. The jasper body ranged from the dry and opaque to the waxen and translucent: that made between 1780 and 1795 feels almost like satin. During the early 1780s a slightly glossy variety was made. Until 1820 texture was fine and uniform of grain and never chalky in appearance. Yet it was porous enough before firing to be stained throughout its substance by mineral oxides to almost any desired colour. Seven ground colours have been noted in snuff-boxes: dark blue, lavender, sage green, olive green and the bluish pink known to collectors as lilac, an intense black and an attractive yellow. These hues varied in tone for technical reasons such

6

as impurities in the oxides used and variations in kiln temperature.

At first the jasper was coloured throughout the mass of its fabric: such snuff-boxes often display spots which appeared during firing. In 1777 Wedgwood discovered that the front of a panel of white jasper could be coloured by dipping into a slip of coloured jasper. From 1780 all snuff-boxes were coloured by this method.

Skilfully worked white jasper embossments were applied to these lustrous coloured backgrounds, against which they stood out clearly in relief. Tiny plaques, cameos and medallions were also made for insertion into the lids of snuff-boxes in ivory, gilded silver, gilt brass and tortoiseshell. Jasper plaques suitable for pocket snuff-box lids measured up to $2\frac{1}{2}$ in. diameter or 2 in. by $1\frac{3}{4}$ in. and cost about sixpence each. The finer of these were protected from damage with a covering of glass.

From originals, moulds were made in plaster of paris or fired potter's clay. The moist white jasper was pressed into such a *pitcher* or intaglio mould until every line and dot was filled. Superfluous clay was then scraped off level with the face of the mould with a modeller's tool. After drying for a few minutes the white jasper relief was extracted, wetted with water and applied by hand to the coloured jasper panel. The reliefs were then tooled and edges undercut to sharpen shadows. The subsequent firing was a skilled operation.

The obvious defects in jasper ware snuff-boxes such as slight warping prompted Wedgwood to use the same technique for their ornament, pressing reliefs separately and applying them to flat panels. His bas reliefs were also set into lids of table snuff-boxes. After 1790 attractive snuff-box lids included tri-coloured specimens, constituting some of the most elaborate of Wedgwood's art work. The ground might be pink, the border blue, and the relief white. The borders enclosing the jasper relief might be reticulated to show the colour of the panel beneath.

Snuff-boxes might be decorated with contemporaneous

portraits classed by Wedgwood as *Heads of Illustrious Moderns*: about a thousand subjects were issued, but few of them on snuff-boxes. The Wedgwood catalogue of 1787 lists 229 names. Portraits are usually in white profile against a blue ground, very occasionally against green or black. The rare full faces include Dr Erasmus Darwin and Flaxman's portraits of Captain Cook, William Pitt and Charles J. Fox. If fitted into a colourful frame of jasper the price of a snuff-box reached one guinea. Snuff-boxes with commissioned portraits were ordered in numbers of not less than ten, usually for presentation purposes and cost three to five guineas each.

John Flaxman, RA, celebrated for his classical work and portraiture, received his first commission from Wedgwood in 1775 and for twelve years produced designs for reproduction in jasper, such as *Muses with Apollo*, 1777. Portraits by Flaxman found on snuff-box lids include George III and his family, Sir Joshua Reynolds, the Duchess of Devonshire and the popular admirals Rodney, Howe, Duncan and St Vincent.

Eliza Meteyard in her *Life of Josiah Wedgwood*, 1865, illustrates a circular table snuff-box set with Flaxman's masterpiece of 1775, *Muses Watering Pegasus in Helicon*. Of this she writes: 'The horse is so instinct with life that it seems to snort and move: and the Muse standing beside it looks as though she lifted her water-bearing vessel to its lips. The life-like attitude of the Muse who seeks to wash the foot of the immortal steed, and of the one who caresses it, are equally remarkable. Even the water breaks into waves. The ornamental setting shows in masterly detail one of the finest borders peculiar to Wedgwood's bas reliefs.'

William Hackwood joined Wedgwood in 1769 and immediately became his leading modeller of bas-relief subjects, some of which are found on snuff-boxes. Josiah Wedgwood considered Hackwood of 'the greatest value in finishing fine small work' suitable for snuff-boxes. He remained with the firm until 1832.

Among the many jasper medallions incorporated into snuff-box lids the more important included: Aurora, the Goddess of the Dawn, 1773; Priam Begging the Body of Hector, 1774; Hercules overcome by Love, 1774; The Philosopher, 1777; Nymph with Garland, 1784; Sacrifices to Victory and other sacrificial subjects.

Jasper reliefs were often set in ormolu or silver mounts thought to have been made by Matthew Boulton. These might be skilfully worked with scrolls or cast with floral sprays and birds. Wedgwood wrote of his jasper cameos that 'these are set in gold and cut steel mountings for snuff-boxes . . . and other trinkets which have lately been much worn by the nobility.'

The facets on hand-wrought cut steel were cut in diamond-shapes, highly burnished and rust-resistant. Most of the remaining examples reflect light as brilliantly today as when they were taken from the wheel. These mountings might also be enriched with an inner fillet of gold, sometimes with the addition of polished jasper ware beads.

Wedgwood jasper snuff-boxes from 1772 to 1780 were impressed *Wedgwood & Bentley* in upper and lower case letters of various sizes: in 1772 he recorded 'going on a plan to mark the whole'. The soft clay beneath the box was impressed with ordinary printer's type of the period, such marks being entirely durable after firing. From 1780 the name *Wedgwood* in any of six varying sizes was impressed.

William Adams, a favoured pupil of Josiah Wedgwood, left his master in 1769 and established a pottery at Greengates, producing jasper snuff-boxes from 1787 to 1805 impressed *Adams*.

Humphrey Palmer of Hanley claimed to have been earlier in the field of jasper reliefs than Wedgwood. But for the impressed marks it would be difficult to distinguish between their work, but Palmer's mounts were probably the work of a Wolverhampton maker. Palmer's modeller cleverly imitated Wedgwood's patterns immediately they appeared in the London shops. Copyright in design was then limited to three months.

John Turner, Lane End, and his son produced from about 1790 some excellent, fine textured jasper, slatey-blue, green and black.

Several snuff-boxes have been noted marked *Mayer*, crudely made of poor jasper.

## POTTERY AND PORCELAIN

The first ceramic snuff-boxes made in England date to the late 1740s and were the work of Thomas Whieldon, Fenton Low, Staffordshire. He improved the existing pottery known as agate ware, variegated throughout its texture with colourful markings and stripes resembling those of the then fashionable agate stone displayed in snuff-boxes and jewellery. The surface of this pottery, glazed by sprinkling with galena, was covered with minute granulations in which snuff tended to accumulate. For the same reason white salt-glazed stoneware was found unsuitable for snuff-boxes: examples seen are of modern manufacture. By using the newly evolved liquid glaze Whieldon produced a smooth surface. He also altered the composition of his agate so that it more closely resembled the real stone.

Whieldon used a white burning clay stained with metallic oxides. By piling flat bats of different coloured clays one upon the other and heavily beating them to drive out enclosed air pockets, he caused the separate clays to adhere to each other in a solid mass. This was cut into slices with wires. This process of laying, beating and slicing was repeated again and again, the run of the grain being preserved. The fine wavy lines of coloured clays were disposed in countless folds with irregular striations giving a picturesque effect yet avoiding violent contrasts. As workmen became skilled in this work the striations became thinner and the effects more attractive.

This mass of vari-coloured clays was almost non-plastic and inclined to split if shaped by throwing on the wheel. The difficulty was overcome by pressing the clay into shaped moulds. After firing the snuff-boxes and lids in their biscuit state were smoothed by hand-polishing and then dipped into the transparent liquid glaze that was introduced in about 1750. By 1760 the glaze was faintly tinged with cobalt, the snuff-boxes then more nearly resembling natural agate. Whieldon sold the units to merchants in Wolverhampton and Birmingham who fitted them into gilded metal mounts, that is, hoops, hinges and spring fasteners. So closely resembling agate stone, these snuff-boxes were in great demand. Eliza Meteyard has recorded that Whieldon also made small oval snuff-boxes painted with flowers on white earthenware.

Snuff-boxes with screw-on covers were among the first articles to be made by the Leeds Pottery. These were in deep cream-coloured pottery and thickly glazed, with an embossed design on the cover. At about this time, the 1760s, snuff-boxes were being made at Bristol in tin-enamelled earthenware decorated in blue, usually painted, sometimes spattered.

Porcelain snuff-boxes in the 18th century were mainly Continental. Factories such as Meissen and Vienna were constant sources of supply in hard paste porcelain from the 1740s, the finer examples set in gold mounts. This porcelain was much tougher than the soft paste porcelains of Bow, Chelsea and Derby which were not strong enough to withstand the strains of snuff-boxes in hourly use. Porcelain snuff-boxes may be found simulating folded letters sealed with red wafers impressed with British coats of arms and inscriptions in English. These are hard paste porcelains from Germany.

English bone china, much stronger than soft paste porcelain, was used for snuff-boxes, which were made in the Staffordshire Potteries from about 1815. Box and cover were fitted into gilt metal mounts such as had been used by the Bilston enamellers. Some were carefully and neatly painted in polychrome enamels; less expensively they were decorated with bat-printed flowers, foliage, shells and the like in black or purple.

Snuff-boxes of the much more durable felspathic earthenware known as stone china were made from about 1815 until the mid-19th century. These were usually decorated in colour under the glaze and were capable of withstanding the rough and tumble of everyday usage.

# CHAPTER 9

# Hardstones

THE COLOURFUL materials used to create individual character in early Georgian snuff-boxes included thin plates of
crystalline hardstones. These were cut and polished and set in
hinged mounts or frames of gold, silver, pinchbeck or one of the
gilded brass alloys. London jewellers assembling these brought
together some of the finest work of the period from gold chasers
and lapidaries.

Agates with their fascinating veins of colour and vitreous
lustre decorated snuff-boxes throughout the 18th and 19th
centuries. This hardstone is immediately recognised by its
flowing colour bands alternating in light and dark colours –
white, yellow, orange, grey or brown. Single colour agate was
also used for snuff-boxes in a variety of tints, mainly by early
Victorian makers. Other varieties of English and Scottish
quartz noted in snuff-boxes include onyx, sardonyx, bloodstone
and cairngorm.

Agates or veinstones, a form of chalcedony, are all more or
less porous and could be stained in vivid colours by soaking in
red, blue, green or brown dye. In addition agate plates, ready
dressed and polished, were imported by the snuff-box makers
from Oberstein, Rhineland. This source was exhausted long
ago but German lapidaries for more than a century have worked
agates from Brazil and other South American states.

Lapidaries in Aberdeen prepared agates from Angus, Mon-
trose and the Ayrshire coast and hardstones from the celebrated
Cairngorm mountains in the Grampian highlands. From here
and three other mountains they obtained quartz crystals in
white, pink, yellow, reddish and dark brown, and black.
These, known to collectors as cairngorms, were found in rock
cavities and among river debris. Of these quartz crystals, the

deep yellow, skilfully cut, were – and still are – sold as Scottish topaz, the darker varieties as smoky topaz. Other native hardstones set in Georgian and Victorian snuff-boxes included porphyry from the Forest of Glenorchy on the Marquess of Breadalbane's Perthshire estate; heliotrope or bloodstone, a dark green chalcedony spotted with red; cornelian, a red chalcedony, stained naturally with oxide of iron.

Derbyshire produced some outstanding hardstones, particularly the blue fluorspar of Castleford with fascinating zig-zags of colour ranging through deep blue, amethyst, tawny brown, pink and honey gold. Derbyshire's marbles in a range of subdued tones were used too. In 1791 William Hutton visited Derby and observed in the shops a wide array of snuff-boxes in Derbyshire marbles and marvelled at their export by the thousand to China and South America. Petrified sponges forming rich patterns are found in stones from the Isle of Wight and the Sussex beaches and these too may be noted in snuff-boxes, cut and polished by local lapidaries.

Perhaps the most highly fashionable of the hardstones imported by the jewellers for setting in snuff-boxes was aventurine. Snuff-boxes set with chrysoprase, a pale green chalcedony mined in Koseinitz, Silesia, became fashionable from about 1740. Mocha stone, an Arabian agate displaying tree-like markings, was set in snuff-boxes throughout the Georgian period. Petrified wood from Austria was also imported by the snuff-box men.

Hardstones were cut on a horizontal wheel of lead dressed with emery powder, a natural mixture of corundum and magnatite, made into a paste with olive oil or water and spread on the flat of the wheel. After grinding, the stone was polished on a tin wheel with tripoli and water, and finished on a zinc wheel with putty of tin and water. Final polishing was carried out by hand and was the work of children. The stones were passed as perfect when water splashed upon their surface made no improvement to the lustre. Stones were polished on both sides so that the interior surface of the box did not clog the snuff.

In many instances snuff-box lids and bases were in hardstone, the mounts being in gold or silver. A fashionable shape was a rectangle or square with clipped corners which required eight vertical side panels of hardstone. Occasionally both lid and base were hinged with a horizontal partition between, intended to contain two qualities of snuff. In another pattern a deep rectangular box was divided centrally with a vertical partition on which hinged a pair of lids. A circular box might be fitted with a cover enriched with a mosaic of vari-coloured agates set in a formal radiating design, each stone separated by a thin, flat ribbon of gold. The central point was emphasised with a contrasting gem such as an amethyst which itself might be encircled with paste diamonds or rock crystal.

Throughout the 18th century there was a demand for the snuff-box carved from a single hardstone, fitted only with a hinged gold mount encircling rim and lid. The earliest hardstone snuff-box of this type recorded so far was mentioned by Francesco Zucchi in 1636. This was made from a solid block of rock crystal. Until about 1750 such snuff-boxes were usually in the shape of escallop shells, although cartouche and trefoil shapes are known as well as circles and oblongs. These stones were for the most part of German origin.

Some London gold chasers traded as specialists in making gold and silver mounts and fitting them with hardstone plaques. George Vertue in 1732 noted that 'of late years in London have been several Chasers of Snuff-boxes' and named Parberry as being 'accounted the best gold chaser' at that time. He referred also to 'a Frenchman named Mr Capheire who died in London *c.* 1710' as a specialist in this work, but rarely is an example found that can pre-date the Queen Anne period.

Until about 1790 hardstone snuff-boxes set with highly polished agates of fine quality might display small masterpieces of the gold chaser's craft, cover and sides being lavishly harnessed with exquisitely worked openwork *à cage*, in gold or silver, the latter usually gilded. Some examples contain recurring motifs of hounds and exotic birds enclosed in a closely scrolled framework all chased in high relief and leaving little of the stone to be seen.

Later came the picture design with mythological subjects incorporating ancient buildings with figures, animals, birds, enclosed in a simple asymmetrical framework of flowers, foliage and C-scrolls. These were more graceful than formerly and less confining of the lustrous hardstone which formed a splendid ground for the precious metal, each enhancing the other. In some snuff-boxes the pictorial design was reflected in the side panels which might form a continuous all-round scene.

From about 1760 the lid mount might extend from the edge of the lid, over the stone in a wide border often depicting birds amidst scrolling floral swags, a matching mount encircling the base of the sides. These mounts were wide and sometimes ostentatious, such as chased floral and acanthus leaves in green gold. Later came narrow mounts pierced and chased with flowers and scrolls hung with garlands, but reeded mounts became more common.

The hardstone plaque set in a snuff-box lid might be further ornamented with a central carved motif such as an ivory or mother of pearl medallion bearing, for example, a classical scene – even profile portraits were fashionable, sometimes signed. From about 1760 to the 1780s it was customary for such appliqué work to be gilded. Carved birds in hardstone of contrasting colour inset with tiny diamonds or other glistening precious stones or gems were considered highly elegant.

For a short period from the early 1740s a series of resplendent snuff-boxes appeared. The lid of light-coloured chrysoprase over pink foil was mounted with carved mother of pearl or ivory with handsome effect. From the early 1770s an oval agate lid might be set with a blue and white jasper cameo such as the Three Graces, Sportive Love, Venus chiding Cupid, the Nine Muses and a hundred others.

Hardstone snuff-boxes of the Georgian period are rarely hallmarked. An Act (12.Geo.II) of 1739 exempted from assay 'snuff-box rims, whereof tops and bottoms are made of stone or shell'. The hallmarks had tended hitherto to deface chased mountings. But the mounts for hardstone snuff-boxes were again required to be assayed from 1797 no matter how elaborate the chasing. For this reason little spectacular work dates later than that year.

A few hardstone snuff-boxes were made during the first quarter of the 19th century, highly effective but with much cheaper openwork in cast silver which might be gilded. This covered lids and sides in all-over designs in the early George II style. The fashion for decorating hardstone covers with appliqué birds and other lively motifs was repeated, with enrichment by innumerable small gems. Hallmarks show that such snuff-boxes were made in white and gilded silver until the 1870s. Another type, usually mistaken for solid silver, was made with mounts stamped by the factory silversmiths and filled with a lead-tin alloy. This was followed by perforated and engraved mounts cut from thin flat silver plate.

Less costly than the Scotch pebbles, as native agates were termed at the time of the Great Exhibition of 1851, were cut and polished blue granites from Aberdeen and Peterhead, used for much small jewellery, sometimes in imitation of intricately inlaid marble, or etched with fluoric acid. Serpentine from the Lizard district of Cornwall, red spotted and white veined, or red veined on an olive ground, was soft and easy to work. By then even the hard rosewood marble from Derbyshire could be cut into plaques for snuff-box lids.

### MARBLE INLAY

An interesting use of hardstones is to be seen in inlay work, the agate, fluorspars, jasper, cornelian and so on being selected for their depth of colour and brilliance. Some light-coloured stones were stained to produce a desirable intensity of hue. These were inlaid in the style of the Italian *pietra dura*, that is, to form a mosaic panel. The English version was developed in Derbyshire during the late 1830s by John Adam of Matlock. Channels were cut into plates of vein-free black marble measuring $\frac{1}{8}$ to $\frac{3}{16}$ in. thick. These depressions, arranged in geometrical and curvilinear patterns, were fitted with colourful marbles or quartzes, sliced and saw-cut to the required shapes, forming gorgeously plumaged birds, vivid butterflies and other insects and sprays of flowers and foliage, among which sprigs of jessamine were notable. The Duke of Devonshire permitted his wonderful collection of Italian stonework to serve as models.

The pieces were embedded in jeweller's cement and rubbed down and polished. Unlike Italian work, this inlay could be finished as a single smooth surface. The extreme delicacy and accuracy of the fitting can only be appreciated by inspection. Eventually, however, Derbyshire inlaid work lost its purely local character in snuff-box lids by including malachite from Russia, soft marbles from Northern Italy and ornamental glass from Venice. Signed examples of such inlay are not infrequent, the name of the maker being engraved in some inconspicuous corner. The names of J. Tomlinson, J. Turner and Selim Bright have been noted.

### FLORENTINE MOSAICS

Snuff-box lids from the 1820s might be set with mosaic pictures constructed from tiny cubes of brightly coloured marble and known as Florentine mosaics. These minute blocks of marble measured about $\frac{1}{32}$ in. long and were laid down and cemented to a flat surface, as a veneer over a base of gold or gilded silver which formed the main surface of the lid. In some instances the surface of the finished mosaic was slightly convex. The marbles were selected in colours to form such scenes as Roman temples, fountains and classical architecture and portraits, animals, birds and flowers. Copies of original Roman mosaic floors were reproduced in miniature. Colours were restricted, resulting in designs being necessarily stiff, although the palette for later mosaics was increased by using dyed tesserae. The earliest

Florentine mosaics displayed on snuff-boxes were the work of Parisian hardstone workers, soon to be rivalled by craftsmen in Naples and Rome. Complete pictorial plaques were imported by English jewellers and mounted into snuff-box lids. Between the early 1850s and the late 1860s Derbyshire marble-men worked Florentine mosaics for Birmingham jewellers. These were more meticulously finished than the Italian imports.

### AVENTURINE

A brownish tinged glass flecked with gold-coloured spangles was used to make snuff-boxes displaying an unusual glittering effect. It was named aventurine when it was discovered by chance by a member of the Venetian glassmaking family of Miotto, early in the 17th century. It was, of course, only an artificial imitation of the form of quartz known as aventurine.

Snuff-box units were exported from Murano to London early in the 18th century when gold chasers fitted them into gold mounts. More than a century passed before Birmingham glass-men were reproducing this artificial aventurine and in the 1850s were selling snuff-box units at about six shillings a pound. Their substance was prepared by fusing for twelve hours a mixture of 300 parts crushed flint-glass and 40 parts iron filings. This when shaped and slowly cooled resulted in an excellent imitation of aventurine. Frequently octahedral flakes of copper were enclosed in a readily fusible glass: according to some authorities the correct name for this is 'gold stone'.

Genuine aventurine is a translucent quartz, yellowish-brownish-red in colour, containing small flakes of glittering mica, which give a gold-spangled appearance to a polished surface in reflected light. This is not known to have been imported until early in the Victorian period. Single stones were cut with flat or slightly rounded surfaces and set into snuff-box lids, gold or silver mounted with substantial rims elaborately chased.

Snuff-boxes were also carved from whitish-reddish-brown

aventurine-felspar flecked with golden particles and known as sunstone. This is much harder than quartz.

### CANNEL COAL

Brittle cannel coal is a bituminous mineral which burns with a bright flame. It is so inflammable that, being lighted with a taper, it burns like a candle and is smokeless: its name is a corruption of candle coal. Known to the Georgians as 'parrot coal', it can be cut and highly polished like jet which it somewhat resembles and is perfectly clean to handle. It is found in the coal seams of Lancashire, Yorkshire and Scotland. A valuable seam was worked in the Wigan coalfield during the 19th century by the Ince Hall Coal & Cannel Co., Wigan.

For nearly two centuries the material was used for snuff-boxes. In 1697 Celia Fiennes visited 'Newcastle Underline [near Wigan] where is the fine shineing Channel Coale . . . that is hard and will be pollish'd like black marble for salts or snuff-boxes or such like, the only difference it will not bear the fire as marble does else it resembles it very much'. James Arbuckle in *Snuff*, a poem written in 1719, refers to snuff-boxes of coal. The *Gentleman's Magazine* reported in 1764 that at Sheffield were made 'snuff-boxes of a sort of coal called kennel, or cannel coal, by Mr Joseph Hancock who is the present Master Cutler'. Hancock was already making snuff-boxes in Sheffield plate. At the Great Exhibition, 1851, carved snuff-boxes in cannel coal were displayed by G. H. Ramsey, Derwent Haugh, Newcastle.

Cannel coal snuff-boxes were fitted with silver mounts and carved in shapes resembling those of contemporaneous hard-stone boxes. The jet black made an excellent ground for gilding: others were painted with floral designs in bright enamel colours fired in a low temperature muffle kiln. Some were coloured with paint. A cartouche-shaped example in the collection of HM Queen Mary, gilded and painted, was made and signed by Joseph Angell, 10, Strand, London.

SLATE

Snuff-boxes of slate proved formidable competitors of Derby-shire marble inlay which had been entirely superseded by about 1860. Slate was so processed that it closely resembled fine marble. It was decorated with black japan and painted in colours with designs adapted from Florentine mosaics. This painting was stoved for several days, making the colours so permanent that pocket friction had no effect. Fitted with electroplated mounts, such snuff-boxes were comparatively inexpensive.

# *Papier Mâché:* Composition:
# Japanned Iron

### PAPIER MÂCHÉ

COLLECTORS of papier mâché snuff-boxes must distinguish between the three products that were made under that name: the original made in London from the 1740s as *papie machie* and in the 19th century as *carton pierre*; paper ware from 1772; and *papier mâché* japanned ware from 1836. Although created by different processes, themselves subject to progressive improvements, the three groups are now classified in collectors' terminology under the single term of papier mâché, a French expression literally meaning 'masticated paper'.

The early Georgian variety, named papier mâché – variously spelt – on a number of London trade cards, consisted of a composition of rags reduced to a fibrous pulp with glue, chalk and fine sand. This was shaped into snuff-box and lid forms by hand pressing into oiled boxwood moulds. When dry these were stoved until hard and then japanned at a low temperature. Die pressing of these forms dates from about 1780.

The papier mâché snuff-boxes preferred by collectors were made by a technique patented in 1772 by Henry Clay, Birmingham. He evolved a process for making a tough, heat and moisture resisting material capable of withstanding the heat of oven japanning to acquire a surface finish which by the 1780s had become as lustrous as oriental lacquer. It was made from sheets of porous textured paper saturated with a mixture of flour and glue. Snuff-box lids and boxes, each as a single unit, were shaped by applying the sheets to a metal mould rather smaller than the required sizes of box and lid. Each layer

33 Silver-gilt
snuff-box in the form
of a mask of Lord
Nelson. The cover is
of oak from H.M.S.
*Bellerophon*, inscribed
'CALVI, Copenhagon,
Trafalgar, Oct. 21.
1805'. Height 3½ in.
In the Victoria and
Albert Museum.

34 Gold snuff-box
presented to Sir
Arthur Wellesley by
the Borough of New
Windsor in 1811.
London hallmark for
1805. Width 3⅜ in.
In the Victoria and
Albert Museum.

35 (*Left*) Silver-gilt snuff-box set with plaque embossed with a horse and lion in a jungle. Maker's mark W.S., Birmingham, 1830. (*Centre*) Triangular snuff-box in silver inscribed with the name JOHN BEAZLEY NEWTON. (*Right*) Silver with an all-over checker design. Maker's mark W P & B S 1800. Bracher & Sydenham.

36 Silver-gilt snuff-box, the cover chased with a view of Battle Abbey, borders of scrolling foliage, the base chased with an unidentified historic building. By Matthew Linwood, Birmingham, 1810.
Christies.

37 Silver snuff-box, the cover chased with a view of Windsor Castle, set against a ground of engine-turning and a chased floral border. By Nathaniel Mills, Birmingham, 1827.
Richard H. Evcrard.

38  Silver snuff-box, the cover chased in high relief with an all-over scene
of a huntsman and hounds in a wood. Base of mother of pearl; engine-turned
sides. By Nathaniel Mills, Birmingham, 1840.
Christies.

39  Silver-gilt snuff-box, chased with the portrait of a greyhound named on
ribbon above. The inscription below reads 'The property of the Earl of Moray.
Gain'd the highest prize at the Downe Coursing Club. Oct.ᴿ 1818'.
Brufords of Exeter.

40  Silver snuff-boxes with engine-turned sides and covers set with chased and
embossed views. (*Top*) Bath and Wells Cathedral by Rawling & Sumner,
London, 1835. 3⅜ in. by 2¼ in. by 1⅛ in. deep. (*Centre*) gilt, with a hunting
scene, by Ledsam Vale & Wheeler, Birmingham, 1828. 3⅜ in. by 2⅜ in. by
⅞ in. deep. (*Bottom*) view of Abbotsford by Francis Clark, Birmingham, 1837.
3 in. by 2 in. by ⅞ in. deep.
Prestons Ltd.

41 Silver table presentation snuff-box with applied flower and foliage decoration. By John Shaw, Birmingham, 1844.
Richard H. Everard.

42 Table snuff-box in 18-carat gold, engine-turned in basket pattern with chased oak leaves and acorn edging in coloured gold. Interior of cover set with a miniature portrait. By A. J. Strachan, London, 1813.
Asprey & Co.

43 Presentation table snuff-box to a major of the 96th Regiment: in the form of a field mess tent with guards.
N. Bloom & Son Ltd.

44 Silver mounted table snuff-box made from a hoof of the cavalryhorse *Midnight*.
N. Bloom & Son Ltd.

45  Silver snuff-box, engraved with carrier's wagon and horses before a village
scene. Maker's mark I H between two stars, 1685. $3\frac{3}{4}$ in. wide.
Victoria and Albert Museum.

46  Gold snuff-box, struck
with the London hallmark
for 1814. Maker's mark
ILWA. Presented to the
Duke of Wellington by the
Borough of Hertford in
1814. $3\frac{1}{16}$ in. diameter.
Victoria and Albert
Museum.

47   Engine-turned gold snuff-box with raised borders, the centre applied with the crowned monogram of George IV in rose diamonds on an oval panel of royal blue enamel. 3¼ in. wide. Marked T B London 1820.
Christies.

48   Presentation snuff-box of tortoiseshell lined with gold. Cover inset with carved portrait of George IV when Regent. The gold cover is chased with the Prince of Wales' feathers and scrolling foliage. The border chased in green-gold with laurel foliage. Inscribed 'The Gift of His Royal Highness George Augustus Frederick, Regent of England, to John Watier, 1815.' 3⅜ in. wide.
Christies.

49  (*Above*) Classical scene
on a silver snuff-box, its
shape and treatment
adapted from the earlier
rococo period. Made in
1823 by William Elliott,
London.
Victoria and Albert
Museum.

50  (*Left*) Silver-gilt 'pedlar'
box, the cover modelled in
high relief with a pedlar of
beverages wearing a plumed
hat, against an engraved
background showing
roisterers outside a tavern.
Maker's mark J.L. London,
1820.
Christies.

51 Four bijou snuff-boxes such as were carried by ladies from 1815. The cover of the example decorated in relief (*third from top*) is cast: the remainder are from rolled plate. The covers are designed with escutcheons in which a crest or cypher could be engraved.
N. Bloom & Son Ltd.

52 Silver-gilt snuff-box, its cover set with a mosaic panel of London origin: the base and sides engine-turned with chased foliage borders and thumbpiece. 2½ in. wide. By Nathaniel Mills, Birmingham, 1835. Christies.

53 Gold and tortoiseshell snuff-box, base and cover piqué posé in gold with birds upon baskets of flowers and fruit, with key pattern borders. The sides are similarly decorated with gardening trophies interspersed with insects. 3 in. wide. Mid-18th century. Christies.

54 Silver snuff-box with cover chased in high relief with a view of Dryburgh Abbey, Scotland, the sides engine-turned with chased foliage borders. 2¾ in. wide. By Joseph Willmore, Birmingham, 1833.
Christies.

55 Silver-gilt snuff-box with rounded ends, cover chased in high relief with three hounds pursuing game amid hills. Base and sides engine-turned. 3¾ in. wide. London, 1824.
Christies.

56 Gold-mounted snuff-box of grey marble, the cover applied with chased gold figures, the surround of gold cage-work pierced and chased. The sides similarly bordered. The cover rim chased with foliage on a matted ground. 3 in. wide. Early 19th century.
Christies.

57 Snuff-box in 18-carat gold with engine-turned panels and shell and foliage thumbpiece. The borders and corners chased with flowers. Struck with the London hallmark for 1825.
Christies.

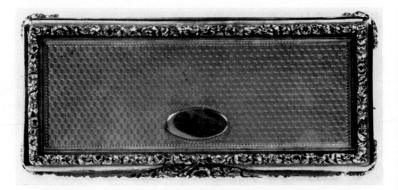

58 A Lancashire *memento mori* pocket snuff-box with hardwood sides and brass plates at top and base. The figure 8 opening ensured that only the smallest pinch of snuff was taken as finger and thumb could not be separated. Dated 1847.

59 A pinchbeck example of the 1750s.

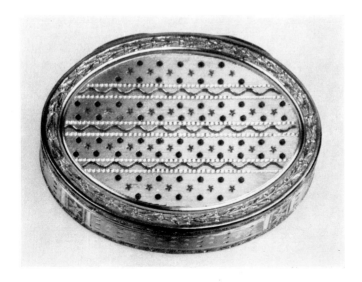

60 (*Left*) Gold snuff-box, centre of the cover inset with a panel of lapis lazuli, the border chased with birds, flowers and scrollwork on a matted ground. The moulded bombé sides similarly decorated on the lower part. Dated 1857. Christies.

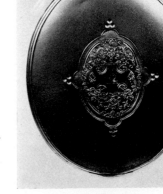

61 (*Right*) Gold snuff-box, the centre of the base and cover chased with scrolling foliage on a matted ground within a shaped oval with pellets at the cardinal points. The interior of the cover set with a miniature portrait. About 1790. Christies.

62 (*Left*) Gold-mounted tortoiseshell snuff-box, the cover set with a gold coronation medal of William and Mary, 1689. Reeded mounts to rim and sides. 3¼ in. diameter. Early 18th century.

63 (*Right*) Gold snuff-box, with engine-turned panel, the border chased with foliage on a matted ground. Centre of the base and cover chased with a swirl of foliage. 2¾ in. diameter. Maker's mark G H London 1798. Christies.

of paper was glued into place and dried at 100° F between each addition. When the correct thickness was reached, the shape was removed from the mould and filed.

A different technique was used for complicated pieces such as the 19th-century shoe snuff-boxes. The paper was applied over a shaped core until half the final thickness was reached. A clean cut was made with a sharp tool, dividing the potential snuff-box into two sections. These were separated and the core removed. The halves were then brought together and several more layers of prepared paper applied. The joint was thus strengthened and made invisible.

Japan varnish was then laid on and the piece stoved at japanner's temperature and undulations removed with pumice stone. This was repeated several times. Black was the most common background but crimson or green was obtained by adding appropriate metallic oxides to the japan varnish. The adhesive used between the sheets of paper was similarly coloured.

The snuff-box was then decorated with colours or gilding, over-painted with clear shellac varnish. This was stove hardened and polished by rubbing with rotten stone and oil. Fine work was given a brilliant silken lustre by women rubbing with their bare hands. This feature is found only on English work.

An excise duty was levied on manufactured paper ware which could be produced only under licence; this ended in 1836. Papier mâché japanned snuff-boxes constructed from machine-made panels date from 1838. The blanks were treated as wood and could be planed and carved: snuff-boxes were assembled from several units. From 1847 this papier mâché was of denser texture.

Paper ware has a flat-smooth texture and is lighter in weight than the later papier mâché which is brittle in comparison and reveals a slightly undulating surface when held in an oblique light.

Decorations until about 1815 were painted in colours often enriched with gilding. Then in 1812 sparkling metallic powders known as bronzes in various colours were patented by Thomas

7

Hubball, Clerkenwell. Within three years pictures and designs on the lids of table snuff-boxes might be composed of bronzes made in about eighteen colours from powdered metals and alloys such as brass, copper, zinc and Dutch metal. Some were chemically stained.

These bronzes were painted over a tacky surface of gold size with wool or cotton waste swabs wrapped around a slender handle. Delicate shading effects and fine lines were painted with a tool made from a fragment of leather tied to a thin string passed through the hollow of a quill so that the leather formed a tiny pad at the tip.

A second bronze period began in 1843, atmospheric effects being obtained by blending gold-coloured bronzes with oil colours. Fascinating lighting effects were created, particularly outdoor scenes with brilliant sunshine. A rare silvery bronze made from powdered aluminium enriched moonlit prospects. Henry Perks painted sumptuous pictures using this technique, signed with a microscopic monogram.

Vividly coloured flowers painted realistically delighted ladies and snuff-boxes so decorated were fashionable from the early 1830s to the 1850s. They were introduced in 1831 by George Neville, Birmingham, who specialised in painting 'flowers on the black'. His signature flower is easily recognised – a blue con-volvulus with one petal curled over in contrasting colour. Other distinctive flower painters were Grimes of Wolverhampton, noted for his snowdrops and hawthorn blossom given glowing brilliance by being painted on a ground of gold or silver leaf. Alfred Harvey was notable for his tiny posies of mixed flowers and W. Wylie was an outstanding all-round flower painter who signed his finest work with a tiny monogram WW. Luke Amner was celebrated for his splendid tulips; William Jackson for lilies of the valley; and William Bourne for the radiance of his verbenas. J. Breakspeare of the firm Jennens & Bettridge, Birmingham, was a skilful mid-century flower painter notable for his miniature adaptations of Dutch old master flower paintings. He taught this industrial art to his son with such success that when the papier mâché trade declined from 1860 he moved to London as a professional artist and became an exhibitor at the Royal Academy.

Frederick Newman became celebrated for the magnificence of his peacocks and William Hamson for his resplendently plumaged parrots. Persian designs on snuff-boxes were created in 1855 by John Hinks of McCullum & Hodgson, Birmingham, and had a five-year vogue. These ornate patterns resembled a Persian carpet, leaf gold outlining vari-shaped spaces filled with vivid colours.

George Evans of Fribourg & Treyer wrote in 1921 describing early 19th-century snuff-boxes with which he was familiar. Their 'lids often bear paintings, subjects generally being landscapes, figure and genre scenes, the latter being often of a coarse nature'. The interiors of some of these box-lids might be painted with nudes or risqué subjects.

There was a considerable demand for 'ceremonial' snuff-boxes after the death of the Prince Consort in 1861. These were decorated in mauve and grey associated with mother of pearl. In 1862 the papier mâché men succeeded in copying hardstone effects at a fraction of the price of the originals. Malachite was introduced in that year by Alsager & Neville, Birmingham, who were also responsible for some superb agate and marble effects, the invention of Peter Jones. Tortoiseshell was also imitated.

Table snuff-boxes in paper ware and japanned papier mâché contributed a delightful radiance to late Georgian and early Victorian homes from about 1815 to the 1850s. A fashionable type made extensively in Wolverhampton and Birmingham, and also imported from Austria and Germany by the thousand, was the circular, flat-lidded box measuring from 4 to 8 in. in diameter and between ½ and 1 in. deep. The lid formed a field for colourful, all-over painting in oils. The early lid had no raised encircling rim, the painting occupying the entire surface. From about 1830 the cover rim was made slightly higher than the flat surface framing the picture in black. All-over paintings are usually the work of more skilful artists than the later series. The paper ware boxes are also more strongly constructed.

The manufacture of such snuff-boxes was a specialist branch of the trade. The majority of covers displayed miniature copies of well-known paintings taken from engravings in colours that could scarcely be considered accurate. The head artist in the workshop would paint a commercial version from which assistants made copies at speed, leaving him to add the finishing touches. On paper ware boxes the collector will sometimes find an original painting: these are highly valued.

An early master painter of such snuff-boxes was Samuel Raven, Birmingham. He is believed to have learned the technique of painting on papier mâché in the workshops of Small & Son, Guest, Chopping & Bill, severing his connection in 1816 when the firm was taken over by Jennens & Bettridge. Raven set up as a freelance painter, but was soon buying snuff-boxes and cigar-cases in the black, decorating them with notable skill and selling them to merchants. After about 1830, in the face of competition from Wolverhampton, his paper ware was of a poorer quality supplied by another firm. Like many another freelance industrial artist Raven was capable of adapting his skill to a wide range of painting techniques to suit the limitations of size and shape imposed by snuff-boxes.

Table snuff-boxes painted by Raven after 1826 are inscribed in red script within the cover *S Raven Pinxt. Patronized by H.R.H. the Duke of Sussex and Prince Leopold of Saxe-Coburg* – sometimes omitting the words 'of Saxe-Coburg'. When the painting is entirely from the hand of Raven it is signed in script so small as to be scarcely visible without a magnifying glass. The title of the picture is inscribed in cream paint.

An apprentice artist employed by Raven from 1820 to 1827 recorded that his master specialised in painting pictures on box lids. During those years he noted that all pictures painted in Raven's studios were copied from engravings. David Wilkie's early works, unprotected by copyright, were popular subjects copied unceasingly. These included *The Blind Fiddler, Rent Dor,*

*Blind Man's Buff*, *The Cut Finger* and *The Village Politicians*.
John Burnet's painting *The Young Bird* and *The Beeswing* by
Kidd were in demand consistently. *The Proposal* and *Congratula-
tions*, after G. H. Harlow and engraved by H. Meyer, were
endlessly repeated by Raven's pupils, who reproduced the
pictures in colours of their own choosing.

In the Victoria and Albert Museum is a grand communal
snuff-box by Raven, excellently painted with Sir Thomas
Lawrence's celebrated portrait of George IV. The interior of
the lid is inscribed *J. Machin/Union Commercial Room/S. Raven
Pinxt.* John Machin became landlord of the Union Inn, Cherry
Street, Birmingham in 1825. Several unsigned examples are
known, usually, but wrongly, attributed to C. H. Stobwasser
& Co., Berlin. Communal snuff-boxes were a feature of the
period in most places where groups of people met; and in the
case of a guild or company were identified by a painted coat
of arms. Even the House of Commons possessed a set. By 1830
the demand for these painted table snuff-boxes had spread to a
wider, less monied public. German imports satisfied their less
discriminating needs and to meet the competition Wolverhampton japanners responded with boxes of the new papier
mâché japanned, cheaper of construction and for the most part
less skilfully painted. The subject of the painted decoration
might be religious, royal, sporting, or a female or theatrical
figure.

A copyist expert in reproducing William Etty's figures was
employed by Edward Perry, Jeddo Works, Paul Street, Wolverhampton and from the 1840s paintings on many lids were
adapted from Titian's *Venus* in the Uffizi Gallery, Florence.
Many copies of R. Westall's *Venus with Doves* came from the
Perry factory. As the custom of offering snuff from table boxes
declined these circular lids were often framed and hung –
usually three lids to a frame.

Line engravings were transfer-printed on inexpensive snuff-
boxes from about 1845. The picture was printed in black oil or
varnish ink on a special tissue paper and transferred to lids of

cream-coloured japan coated with a special varnish. The line engraving, showing clearly against the light surface, was then coloured and gilded. Finally the picture was coated with transparent varnish, a brilliant lustre being secured by rubbing with a woollen cloth dipped in mastic. Later it became customary to paste a paper disc with a printed engraving to the lid.

William and Andrew Smith of Mauchline (see page 124) from the early 1850s made wooden snuff-boxes japanned and decorated in imitation of papier mâché.

Papier mâché snuff-boxes were not long-lasting, the hinge attachments being weak spots. Collectors should be aware that papier mâché snuff-boxes have been reproduced. Close comparison with an original will show that these fakes have not been japanned, varnished, stoved and polished by the appropriate old methods and the paints differ in quality and brush work. Fingers travelling lightly over the glossy surface will meet with undulations absent from original paper ware.

## COMPOSITION

Obadiah Westwood of Birmingham evolved and patented in 1785 a process for making a tougher, harder composition to supersede the earlier pressed *papie machie* (see page 96). Westwood's method consisted of 'cutting and bruising or grinding rags (linen, silk, hemp, flax or cotton) until of a fine texture which are then mixed with a strong paste of glue, flour and water'. Into this was kneaded a small quantity of colouring matter such as Spanish brown, red lead, umber or black. After varnishing and stoving this composition displayed a really fine surface finish resembling japanned work, but was much less costly to produce. Snuff-boxes pressed from this composition continued in production for more than sixty years.

Snuff-boxes with views embossed upon the lids with boxwood moulds in the style of early 19th-century silver were made in tens of thousands annually and bore a superficial resemblance to pressed horn. They were fitted with narrow metal-gilt mounts. Impressions on the lids were very clear until about 1850 when they began to deteriorate. The boxes were all rectangular or oval in shape and weighed about three ounces.

Early composition boxes might be more elaborate and examples have been noted with lid, sides and base inlaid with gold and silver such as trophies of arms and cyphers. The lid of an example sold at Christies in 1967 was fitted with a silver-gilt mount set with a Florentine mosaic (see page 22) of a spaniel beneath a tree stump, attributed to about 1800.

### JAPANNED IRON

Japanned snuff-boxes date from late in the 17th century. The parish registers of Bilston, Staffordshire, record several births dating from 1702 onwards in which the fathers were described as makers and decorators of japanned snuff-boxes. These boxes were in hammered iron plate, circular, oval or oblong with pull-off lids, usually black with some gilding. Similar snuff-boxes were already being manufactured in Sheffield and by about 1720 the trade had extended to Wolverhampton. These snuff-boxes, sold by the 'snuff houses' at about threepence each, are now extremely rare. They may be recognised by the slightly undulating surfaces of the heavy gauge iron plate.

The second group of japanned iron snuff-boxes dating between the late 1720s and the 1780s were made from heavy gauge tin plate rolled into thin sheets, even surfaced on both sides. This was iron soaked in molten tin which penetrated its texture and gave the metal a silvery white colour. Pure grain tin from Cornwall was used in the form of shot. This process gave a slight radiance to the japanner's ground colours. The finest snuff-boxes of this period were made by the Allgood family of Pontypool. They developed a process which gave the japan and its decoration a highly durable, granite-hard surface, lustrous and silky to the touch. Pontypool also made snuff-boxes of apanned copper, wi th hinged lids.

Tortoiseshell snuff-boxes (see page 116) were fashionable

throughout the George II period. Japanners of Pontypool and Birmingham produced snuff-boxes decorated to imitate tortoise-shell. These were inexpensive and the demand was considerable. Robert Dossie in 1754 reported that the tortoiseshell effect was 'not only the japanned ground for snuff-boxes and other small pieces, but was also decorated with painting and gilding in the same way as any other varnished surface and which is best done after the ground has been duly hardened by the hot stove: but it is well to give a second annealing with a more gentle heat'. Dossie added that this stoving required to be continued for three weeks or a month. The japan was applied over silver leaf or a white ground. This was clouded and stained with yellow to resemble tortoiseshell. It was given numerous coats of clear varnish, each being stoved.

An inferior quality was made at Wolverhampton, circular splashes of gold and silver leaf being immersed beneath semi-transparent yellow or crimson japan. Against this tortoiseshell effect ornamental motifs were painted in colour such as flowers, fruit or foliage.

Early Pontypool snuff-boxes were also japanned in chocolate colour and the celebrated glowing crimson which was given its impeccable finish by applying gold or silver leaf over a white ground. The Pontypool palette was extended from the late 1770s to include dark green, puce, tomato red, orange, canary, grey and ultramarine blue. But by 1760 Wolverhampton and Birmingham were japanning snuff-boxes in yellow, vermillion, red, lake, blue, indigo, green, brown, purple and flesh white. Not until about 1820 was an improved green japan made: this was costly and is found only on snuff-boxes of the highest quality, often with a basis of block tin.

In 1756 Bishop Pocock visited the Pontypool workshops and noted in his diary that they 'adorned all kinds of boxes with Chinese landscapes and figures in gold only, and not with the colours as Birmingham. This [Pontypool] ware is very much better than the Birmingham, but it is dear', an opinion expressed in 1781 by the Hon. John Byng who recorded in his diary:

'Chepstow. I bought a Pontypool snuff-box, a beautiful and dear ware much to be admired.'

Decorations were now painted in full colour, mainly rustic groups incorporating figures of shepherds and woodmen, and sporting subjects. The celebrated artist Thomas Barker of Bath was born at Pontypool where he was for a few years employed by the Allgoods as a painter of scenic views on snuff-boxes and trays.

The third group of japanned snuff-boxes consisted of boxes made from tin iron plate invented in 1784 by a Wolverhampton ironmaster specially for the use of japanners. This was made from best bar iron in which charcoal was an ingredient instead of coke. This increased malleability enabling it to be rolled to a thinner gauge than formerly. The shaped boxes and their lids were scoured by women and stored in tubs of water until such time as they could be dipped in molten grain tin. Only the surface of the iron was coated with a film of tin, resulting in a great saving of the costly metal.

When hinged mounts were fitted to japanned snuff-boxes they were of cast brass, gilded. From about 1795 mounts might be cast in soft leaded pewter disguised by mercury gilding.

# CHAPTER II

# Horn: Scottish Mulls

## HORN

CHEAP, tough and extraordinarily adaptable, for centuries horn was one of the basic materials in the English home. Whether his need was a window or a button, an inkwell, a comb, a tip to his bow, or, from early in the 17th century, a snuff-box, the Englishman called upon the ancient, specialised skills of that little-lauded craftsman, the horner. Master horners tended to occupy small workshops, often employing only members of their own families. Because of 'the grete and corrupt stench' emanating from their premises 'to the grevous annoyance of neighbours', London horners in 1455 were directed to transfer their workshops to the city outskirts. They selected the Petticoat Lane district with which they were continuously associated for more than four hundred years.

Snuff-taking until late in the 17th century was mainly a plebeian custom. It was found that horn boxes made the most suitable and inexpensive containers for the finely powdered 'tobacco-snuff', a term then used to distinguish it from various popular herbal snuffs such as crushed camomile flowers. Two distinct branches of the horner's craft were recognised. These were the horn pressers who prepared the green or raw horn and pressed it into plates of convenient thickness, and the moulders who bought unused tips and roots of horn and scraps from the pressers. Until the 1660s the supply of horns from tanners and butchers fully met the needs of the trade. By the end of the century buffalo and other horns were imported from America. In 1696 John Houghton estimated that the horns of 350,000 beasts were needed annually to satisfy the twenty-four master horners then operating in London.

There was a great demand for the horns of Scottish rams from about 1700. When processed these displayed an amber tint and could be easily dyed in attractive shades of red, green, blue and brown. A jet black, which could be highly polished, was achieved by sanding the horn snuff-box and painting it with 50 or 60 grains of nitrate of silver dissolved in one ounce of distilled water. This was colourless. When dry the boxes were placed in the sunlight where they soon turned jet black.

The *Dictionarium Polygraphicum*, 1735, described the process of 'casting horn in a [brass] mould like lead. Make a lixivium of calcin'd tartar and quick lime; into this put scrapings of horn; boil them well together in a copper cauldron of hot water until they come to a pulp; tinge this with what colour you would have it and you may afterwards cast it in a mould and make of it anything of what form you please'.

The horn presser made his plates from the central portions taken from the horns of English cattle, clear and free from striations and other blemishes. The horns were boiled until soft and malleable, then split lengthways with a curved knife and immediately pulled open with a pair of broad-bladed tongs held by another worker. These strips were then placed beneath heavy stones which held them flat until cold. They were then re-softened in the boiling cauldron and each was placed between two iron plates smeared with grease and of considerably greater area. A number of these were pressed vertically into a trench dug in the ground. At one end a narrow space was left for inserting a wooden wedge which was hammered down with a heavy wooden beetle, thus forcing the iron plates against the pieces of horn which gradually expanded into flat plates. After being pressed as tightly as possible they were left in position until cold. These plates were bought by snuff-box makers for cutting into suitable strips.

Until the 1660s the majority of horn snuff-boxes were made from plain-surfaced plates. Then came the vogue for impressing the lids with coats of arms, portraits of royalty and celebrities, classical and sporting scenes. Trimmed sections of sheet horn were softened in cauldrons of hot water and impressed with relief ornament by means of steel moulding tools. The impression needed to be taken quickly to ensure that the relievo was sharp and clear in outline. Oval and circular snuff-boxes were preferred, but rectangular boxes were made also, the two sides folded vertically in a piece, the ends incurved and welded whilst soft. The sides usually remained plain but could be decorated by carved, incised or pressed work. In some instances the horners produced spiral grooves by winding a copper wire around the box whilst it was soft.

Several workers in this medium are known to have engaged in the ornamental pressing of horn, but apart from John Obrisset their reliefs tended to be blurred. Obrisset (d. 1731), son of an émigré Huguenot ivory carver from Dieppe who settled in London and Anglicised his name, followed his father's skills in ivory and eventually became an engraver of ivory, the term then denoting one who carved. But he specialised in sinking steel dies with patterns to be impressed in relief upon small tablets of horn and tortoiseshell suitable for use as snuff-box lids, also supplying similar dies to silversmiths. Obrisset was not an approved silversmith, however, for his mark was not registered at Goldsmiths' Hall.

He specialised in portraiture, usually profile busts or full-length equestrian figures, and for a quarter of a century was acknowledged as a craftsman of outstanding ability. Little is known of his personal life but he was twice married, first in 1690 and secondly in 1717 to Susanne Brisson, the register describing him as of St Martins in the Fields. Formerly he had occupied workshops in Wheel Street, Spitalfields. Contemporaneous records in the possession of the Huguenot Society refer to the family as 'a middling sort of people'.

Much of Obrisset's work was signed, usually with the initials OB or I OB, often accompanied by three, five or seven petalled flowers. A few were impressed with his name in full, some being a combination of OB in capitals and the remainder of his name in script at a period when silversmiths used the first two letters of their surname when marking Britannia standard silver. Six patterns have been recorded with dates, the earliest being a portrait of Queen Anne, 1705. Her consort, Prince George of Denmark, appears on a box impressed I * OB * F *1708*; the Drake box is impressed *John Obrisset Fecit 1712*; a negro's head, with a slave's collar encircling his neck is impressed · 1720 · OB · FECIT. The equestrian portrait of George II dated 29 October, 1727, commemorated the king's attendance at the Lord Mayor's banquet. This function took place, however, on the 30th, the king's birthday. The last of his dated pieces was a sporting subject impressed *De^{bre} · 14 · 1728 OBrisset*, the six final letters in script. Lid interiors might be pressed with the initials OB suggesting that John Obrisset was at once the die-sinker, horn worker and craftsman who made the box.

With very few exceptions Obrisset's horn snuff-boxes have an even surface on the underside of the lid, a few being slightly concave; inner and outer surfaces of the base are smooth and even. Rims are usually without metal mounts, the cover being attached by a flanged hinge riveted to one of the long sides. The portrait or other design is usually rimmed with a pressed border, plain or scrolled.

The relief design from 1715 might be framed in a silver mount hinged to the rim and usually reeded. The curved hinge attached with silver pins to the oval or circular box projected outwards by as much as $\frac{3}{16}$ in. and was liable to catch on the fabric of the pocket until special wash-leather snuff-pockets were introduced. A strengthening plate of thin tortoiseshell might be fitted against the hinge inside the lid. A thumbpiece for lifting the lid was fitted opposite to the hinge. Another design had vertical or slightly bombé sides of silver: the base, at this time, was of tortoiseshell. Boxes wholly of silver have been noted, the lid set with a horn portrait and a plain inner lid of ivory. The silver might be double gilt, but this is now badly worn. In some instances a pair of pressed plaques were fitted as lid and base of a snuff-box.

One series of Obrisset snuff-boxes have flat lids mounted centrally with cast and chased silver portraits in high or low relief, against matted grounds. Silver relief work might also cover the entire field such as the several versions of Charles I in plain armour. On other boxes the portraits were struck from very thin silver plate. The silver used was of the high or Britannia standard quality from 1697 to 1720 when there was a reversion to sterling.

Obrisset's subjects were for the most part profile portraits and full-length equestrian figures in armour; often the ground was matted. Many were adapted from the works of medallists, portraits of English monarchs from James I to George II being a speciality. Snuff-boxes displaying portraits of the Stuart Charles I, his consort Henrietta Maria, and James II were carried by Jacobites. His bust of Charles I was adapted from a medal engraved by John Roettiers: seven variations have been collated, all signed OB.

The monarchs Queen Anne and George I appeared on many Obrisset snuff-boxes. Queen Anne was engraved at least twenty-five times, each with a minor variation. One has the base of the box pressed with the Garter Star, centrally placed, its pointed rays extending to the rim. George II, taken from the medallion portrait of Ehrenreich Haninbal, master of the mint at Clausthal-Zellerfeld, Hanover, was made to commemorate his accession in 1727. Collectors also value jugate portraits of William III and Mary II and such subjects as Prince William of Denmark, Queen Caroline, Philip V of Spain, Peter the Great, the Duke of Marlborough and Oliver Cromwell.

Snuff-boxes with the arms of Sir Francis Drake impressed in sharp relief are met with in several variations each of which required a fresh die to be sunk. It is probable that the earliest were issued as souvenirs commemorating the death in 1696 of Drake, the first Englishman to circumnavigate the world. They were in demand by seamen and other frequenters of waterside inns and taverns displaying such signs as Sir Francis Drake, Admiral Drake and the Drake Arms. This accounts for the fact that so many existing specimens are in common horn. These are often offered as historical relics purporting to have been the personal property of Sir Francis and have long been exhibited as such, despite the large number in existence. A series of exquisitely embossed Drake snuff-boxes are marked *John Obrisset Fecit 1712*: two examples are in the British Museum. Lady Elliott-Drake in 1911 recorded that these presentation boxes were made to the commission of the third baronet who was a candidate in the Taunton parliamentary election of 1713.

Obrisset also issued Biblical subjects such as the conversion of Saint Paul after the relief by Sir Francis Bird on the pediment of St Paul's Cathedral. This was pressed in 1710 to commemorate the opening of Wren's new cathedral building. A silver-mounted oval snuff-box in the British Museum is signed * OB * ACTES YE IX X.

Snuff-boxes exist displaying evidence of long and vigorous use, the relief work virtually obliterated by pocket friction. This defect is not apparent on patch-boxes, counter-boxes and bonbonnières made by Obrisset in horn or tortoiseshell.

Horn snuff-boxes produced by craftsmen impossible to identify might have their covers enriched with colour. These include: gilded designs incorporating birds, insects and beasts within foliage borders; relief work heightened with gilding; faceted lenticular crystals, agates, cairngorms or other native stones set in the centre; ivory medallions similarly set, these being engraved with cypher or inscription. From about 1750 engine-turning, too, might be introduced.

From the mid-18th century snuff-boxes were made from horn shavings ground into powder, then softened by boiling in strong potash lye. The resulting paste was moulded into the required shape by tools in a fly press. When dry the box was polished by rubbing with subnitrate of bismuth applied on the palm of the hand. Shapes and sizes of snuff-boxes made in this way for more than a century are too numerous to collate. However, temperature variations caused these moulded horn snuff-boxes to become speckled and mildewed and quickly crumble so that few of them remain.

### SCOTTISH MULLS

Snuff-taking was a well-established social custom in Scotland from the late 16th century, originally valued for its supposed medicinal virtues such as curing catarrh, tooth-ache and 'naughty breath'. Scottish snuff at this time contained no tobacco, consisting of the dried and powdered leaves of *Achillea ptarmica*, a member of the yarrow family known by the 1590s as sneezewort and long used as a sternutatory. To the Scotsman this herbal powder was known as *sneeshin* and to take a pinch of snuff was *sneesing*. Macgill in *Old Ross-shire*, 1659, alludes to a 'sneeshin maker' named Walter Denune. Howell in his *Letters* of the same year noted that sneeshin 'mightily refreshed the brain,' adding that 'one shall commonly see the [Scottish] serving maid upon the washing block, and the swain upon the ploughshare when they are tired with labour, take out their boxes of sneeshin and draw it into their nostrils with a quill; and it will beget new spirits in them, with a fresh vigour to fall to their work again'. Hall in 1761 differentiated between tobacco snuff and the herb sneeshin: 'I have sent you a little Provision of the best Preston-Paris snuff with a bottle of Highland Snishon.'

Highlanders who accompanied the Court of James I to London in 1603 introduced the sneeshin miln, known to collectors as a snuff-mull, following a Scottish pronunciation of mill. This has always been made from a ram's horn, the point curled artificially into a scroll to prevent it from rubbing a hole in the pocket or bag. The exterior of the horn, sometimes stained black, was scraped smooth and highly polished and the interior cut vertically with closely spaced sharp ridges. These abrading edges enabled the snuff-taker to grind his own snuff from a plug of tobacco or sneeshin.

The rim of the horn was usually fitted with a hinged cover of horn; from the 1670s the cover might be of silver or pewter with an upward-curving thumbpiece. This was most usually plain but often enriched with a centrally placed facet-cut gemstone excavated from the Scottish mountains, such as light or dark cairngorm, colourful agate or transparent crystal. On silver the gem was usually encircled with thistles or foliage embossed in high relief. In Georgian examples the surface of the horn was carved with an ornamental motif, subjects ranging from a laughing Scotsman with long hair and bonnet or a thistle between a pair of leaves, to a duck or an elephant's head.

Differentiation between the Georgian snuff-mull and snuff-box continued. In 1771 Tobias Smollett noted: 'The lieutenant pulled out, instead of his own Scottish mull, a very fine gold snuff-box.' From about 1760 and throughout George III's reign snuff-mulls might be carved from ivory, bone or wood, the latter often displaying the laughing Scotsman motif. By this time serrations within the horn were no longer required by those who bought ready-ground tobacco snuff or sneeshin.

Many a Scotsman, from about 1700, carried with his snuff-mull a tiny spoon, instead of a quill, for applying the snuff to his nose, and a hare's foot for wiping his upper lip afterwards. These were attached to the lid mount by fine chains of silver.

The pocket snuff-mull measured between 1¾ in. and 3½ in. overall, but the collector finds the same design on a more lavish scale in the table snuff-mulls constructed from the horns of highland cattle. These were designed for communal use in the home, tavern or club, richly appointed specimens being intended for guild ceremonies and masonic banquets. Such a table snuff-mull, with a tortoiseshell cover and silver mounts, was sold at Christie's in July 1968. Originally this was the property of the Crossgates Chicken Pie Club, founded in 1760 with the object of improving the breed of horses and cattle. For seventy-four years members met over suppers of chicken pie and in May 1834 became incorporated with the Dunfermline Agricultural Society.

Shaped in a bold spiral of one-and-a-half turns and measuring 8 to 10 in. in height, as much as 18 in. overall and 3 in. wide at

8

the mouth, the table snuff-mull was fashionable from late in the 18th century to the 1860s. Its use was restricted to the service of good quality tobacco-snuff. The oval mouth of the horn was fitted with a capacious snuff-box of silver, its lower edge attached to the rim with silver pins concealed beneath a circuit of beading or reeding. The cover was hinged and fitted with a narrow thumbpiece, plain multi-scrolled or with a scalloped edge. The cover was usually topped by a figure in the round cast in solid silver, such as a Highlander, lion or horse, or an eagle with outspread wings alighting on its kill. This was commonly used as a handle for lifting the lid. On fine examples from about 1820 a ball and tongue hinge was fitted; otherwise a plain five-lug butt hinge was used. An identifying shield-shaped plaque was usually applied to the horn below the box, but might be replaced by an embossed thistle flower between a pair of leaves.

The long conical end of the mull was fitted with a protecting sheath, usually of smoothly plain silver with an applied edge matching that of the box. A paw or ball foot was attached to the outer curve of the horn below the box by means of an expansive lion or other mask. This gave stability to the mull and permitted it to be pushed smoothly across the table. Attached to the lower part of the mount by slender silver chains might be a snuff spoon, hare's foot, pricker, rake and mallet. All the silver mounts and accessories might be gilded.

Table snuff-mulls from early in the 19th century might be mounted with Sheffield plate, the finials in solid silver; from 1835 in British plate (silver fused to a nickel alloy); and from the late 1840s in electroplated silver on copper.

Ram's head table snuff-boxes, also, are associated with Scotland. The skulls, richly ornamented with silver and Scottish gemstones, became a fashionable conceit from about 1840. An example made by Walter Baird, 72 Argyle Street, Glasgow, shown at the Great Exhibition, 1851, was catalogued as 'a Scotch ram's head, each horn measuring 3 ft 5 in., mounted as a snuff-box and cigar case, in gold and silver, adorned with a cairngorm and Scotch amythyst stones'. Another, made by M. McGregor, Perth, was mounted with a silver snuff-box on top of the skull with a full set of accessories, the end of each horn carrying a thistle-shaped mount set with a Scottish amethyst.

# CHAPTER 12

# Tortoiseshell: Piqué: Mother of Pearl

## TORTOISESHELL

TORTOISESHELL in warm translucent yellows and amber tones finely mottled with brown tints made fashionable snuff-boxes and other minor personal accessories in Stuart England. The craft of working tortoiseshell into sheets and moulding it into relief patterns had long been understood by English jewellers. This delightful shell exists as a surface layer on the back of the hawksbill sea turtle (*Testudo imbricata*) found off the Brazilian coast. The shell, weighing five to 25 lb according to size, is separated from the turtle's external skeleton by placing smokeless fire beneath it. The plates then lift from the bone and may be levered off with a long knife. Tortoiseshell of inferior quality is taken from the *Testudinata* which produce five large horn-like plates from the middle of the carapace or shell and four smaller scales from each side. These are known commercially as blades. In addition there are 25 smaller scales, known as feet or noses, taken from the margin.

The material consists mainly of a substance resembling gelatine, with a small quantity of inorganic matter. It is found as naturally compressed cells, but under heat and potash these become spherical. The shell then becomes plastic and may be shaped, pressed or moulded as desired, these forms being retained when cold.

Tortoiseshell was welcome for snuff-boxes because the powdered snuff did not cling to its smooth surface. It could be embossed in screw moulds after softening by immersion in boiling salted water, the pattern being impressed with tools cut in intaglio as with horn. Hunting and genre scenes, floral and scrollwork patterns, geometric designs, masonic and other devices were all popular.

Pocket snuff-boxes were constructed from sheet tortoiseshell rarely more than $\frac{1}{8}$ in. thick: table snuff-boxes were stronger, the plate measuring about $\frac{3}{16}$ in. thick. Pieces of shell could be welded together by the application of low heat from smokeless court charcoal, later from peat charcoal. Heat tends to darken tortoiseshell, hence a low temperature is essential. Seams are invisible. The material had to be handled gently, however. Horace Walpole noted the risk of sudden disaster when he commented to George Selwyn, in a letter of 3 August 1760, 'Hearts do not snap like a tortoiseshell snuff-box'.

All-over incised ornament on the thin tortoiseshell was introduced by Matthew Boulton in the mid-1760s when he was commissioned to make several engine-turning lathes for Josiah Wedgwood. He then manufactured them for sale. With this machine tortoiseshell could be cut with intricate patterns.

The lids of tortoiseshell snuff-boxes were often enriched with elaborate designs in gold, but more usually the plain, handsomely grained shell was considered adequately decorative. This was dark in colour until the 1770s when honey-blonde shell became fashionable.

A long series of tortoiseshell snuff-boxes made between the 1770s and about 1820 even lacked metal mounts, consisting wholly of shell, the lid fitting securely over the box opening and including a tortoiseshell thumbpiece for lifting. Lids might be decorated with pressed work, in contrast to engine-turning beneath the base. A favourite all-over pattern was basket-work.

During the first quarter of the 19th century oblong snuff-boxes with clipped corners and ribbed or slightly concave sides were fashionable, with plain gold mounts and ornament in gold lines. The cover might be of plain, attractively marked blonde tortoiseshell or might be set with a cast gold or gilded silver plaque displaying a profile portrait in low relief, subjects including royalty and naval, military and political celebrities. Other plaques were of ivory painted with miniature portraits, classical subjects or scenes in colour; mother of pearl exquisitely carved with ornamental subjects; fine stoneware known as jasper usually in blue with relief decoration in white. The plaque was usually framed in a narrow gold fillet and often protected by glass (see under *Piqué*).

Large tortoiseshell snuff-boxes for table and mantelshelf were made from sheet tortoiseshell made by welding together pieces of shell by the application of smokeless heat so that seams were invisible. Motifs in relief could be saw-cut separately by hand and punched into the softened shell and welded into position, giving a three-dimensional effect to the design on the lid, comparable with the period's embossed silver, while the sides were decorated with all-over patterns in relief. Only when held against the light can this welding be detected as irregularities of pattern fail to correspond with surface markings.

## PIQUÉ

The fine texture and translucency of tortoiseshell made it a splendid material to be lit with touches of gold. Scintillating effects were achieved by piercing the shell with tiny metal rods of graduated sizes until the surface appeared to be dusted with golden spangles outlining human figures, exotic birds, insects, flowers, vine patterns, peculiarly elaborate escallop shells, coronets and monograms. This notion was created late in the 17th century by one Laurentini, a jeweller of Naples. France and England adopted the craft so skilfully that it is known today in both countries by its French name, *piqué*. There is no English term for this exotic decoration. Light delicate work is known as *piqué d'or*. Patterns in large points were given the name of *clouté d'or* or nail head piqué; *foulé point d'or* consisted of points crowded into intricate patterns.

The term *piqué posé* is now applied to the style more exactly known by its old name of inlay. In this the ornament is more emphatic, being formed with inlays of strip gold or silver, sometimes still with the piqué patterns for background diaper, trellis work and leaf outlines among the heavier solid scrolls. Occasionally a really elaborate snuff-box may be inset with solid panels closely chased with shells or similar detailed relief work set off by delicate many-pointed shells of gold inlay surrounding diapers in different sizes of gold piqué so that the whole gold-lined box – lid and sides and even base – possesses a mellow, golden glow far richer and lovelier than solid gold. It is possible to find a piqué d'or snuff-box with minor flower borders around a splendid peacock outline in the smallest size of gold points with six or more sizes of point upon its tail.

Some of the earliest piqué was applied to snuff-boxes of both tortoiseshell and ivory, sometimes with matching watch cases. Both made excellent vessels for snuff, preserving its varying delicate aromas more perfectly than any metal except gold, seldom warping to spill in the pocket or fail to open in the hand and offering constant delight to fingers and eye.

Advertisements in the *London Gazette* in 1700 for stolen property included two piqué snuff-boxes: 'a round Tortoiseshell Gold studded Snuff-Box with a Gold joint' and 'a large Gold Snuff-Box, the outside Tortoiseshell with Gold Studs, and the inside solid Gold'. These and other advertised descriptions suggest that piqué point was the more usual technique. Then fashion demanded the many variants of palmettes and strapwork in piqué posé.

A collection of piqué snuff-boxes pre-dating 1715 may include an extensive range of design adapted from those of contemporaneous precious metals, cartouche and shell shapes figuring considerably. An early snuff-box may open with a small drop hinge but the projecting pin hinge came into use early in the 18th century, high quality of craftsmanship being a feature of English piqué. Even the plainest repetition of these points of light distributed evenly over the surface of the tortoiseshell created an effect of shimmering restrained beauty.

By early Georgian days posé d'or was being used alone. Some specimens may appear almost overladen with golden chinoiserie scenes and figures among pillared ruins, pastoral and hunting groups, pavilioned gardens, tea parties and music parties and cloud-borne cupids in scroll and leaf borders. Even the Paris balloon ascent of 1773 has been commemorated on blonde tortoiseshell snuff-boxes. Often the gold mounts are chased, a refinement that adds greatly to the delicacy of the effect.

The English piqué craftsmen developed hairline posé d'or in the early 18th century. Seascapes and other pictorial scenes were achieved in lines of gold or silver as delicate as pen drawing, subjects becoming more elaborate in the early 19th century. Such work on snuff-boxes is uncommon.

Gold and silver for piqué work were used in a pure state without any alloy whatsoever. The metal was thus soft enough to be rolled or beaten to paper thinness. Cut to shape it was pressed upon the surface of tortoiseshell heated by court quality charcoal, then tool-worked into position. The contraction of the tortoiseshell in cooling held it firmly in place without jeweller's cement which would mar the clarity of the inner surface of the shell. The surface was made perfectly smooth by scraping away superfluous tortoiseshell, then polishing and burnishing the whole. The metal was so soft and thin that it could be shaped by hand tools over embossed tortoiseshell, but in this case a hard varnish adhesive was used. For hairline piqué posé a thin shallow groove was cut into the heated tortoiseshell, the strip of metal was inserted into this and given a light hammer blow. When the shell cooled it was held permanently in position. In ivory the piqué work was hand-tooled into the surface and fixed by a cement.

The majority of piqué snuff-boxes found today reflect the change to more formal patterns in the second half of the 18th century. One or two pseudo-classical motifs might be developed with exquisite delicacy – such as an oval patera with a swag of husks on a plain oval box or a conventional honeysuckle flower or an urn flanked by loops of drapery. The ellipse or oval with pointed ends was popular in the late 18th century. Lids were usually piqué edged with cable pattern with a posé motif at their meeting points. In the centre might be a miniature portrait framed in piqué posé, an oval patera, or a silver panel engraved with the owner's crest.

Such pioneers of factory silversmithing and jewellery as Matthew Boulton included piqué work among their manufactures. In a letter to James Adam in 1770 Boulton confirmed that production was in progress and ten years later he acquired the workshops of John Gimblet, a considerable maker of fine piqué posé who operated at Snow Hill, Birmingham, from the early 1760s to 1780.

Substantial gold inlay continued as a successful branch of the Birmingham and Sheffield factory trade well into the 19th century. One result was that the hand-craftsman in piqué turned to ivory as the loveliest gold stud work of piqué d'or was developed more extensively than formerly on this equally inviting surface, often vividly stained green, red, blue or black which set off the points of gold or silver. This work continued through the late 18th and early 19th centuries.

Star ornament is characteristic of this period, probably adapted from the French hand-workers, but popular with the factory piqué men of Birmingham. The sprig pattern was usually associated with factory worked stars and small double circles until about 1800. Some heavy nail head or *clouté piqué* suggests Boulton craftsmanship, the star-head facets shaped by hand as in his cut-steel work: in Victorian specimens from 1872 they were machine-worked. Designs on ivory in posé d'or were seldom in more than simple line work. No signed piqué snuff-boxes have been recorded.

Imitations of piqué snuff-boxes were made during the late 19th century. These are in celluloid, cleverly simulating tortoiseshell and decorated with gilt nail heads and stars fixed with adhesive. Sooner or later one falls away, revealing the deception.

### MOTHER OF PEARL

The splendid opalescence of mother of pearl snuff-boxes was acknowledged by Georgians of the 1790s and early 1800s, a period when precious metals suffered from war-time scarcity. In addition to their fascinating chromatic effects these snuff-boxes were a delight when opened, when the inner pearly surfaces of the shell panels were revealed, for the metal setting was restricted to narrow mounts, usually of silver-gilt.

The mother of pearl for boxes came from the linings of three varieties of haliotis shell, known to manufacturers as great snails, ear shells and buffalo shells. After being sawn into convenient sections the pieces were flattened on a horizontal grinding wheel, smoothed with a mixture of pumice stone and pumice powder, and given their final brilliance with buff leather and rotten stone. This was the work of craftsmen who took a pride in finding shells which could be cut in series of matching panels. The *London Directory*, 1797, lists about twenty master-men in the pearl trade who worked upon the delicate substance with saws, files, drills and sulphuric acid. There was a revival of mother of pearl snuff-boxes during the early Victorian period by the pearl workers of Birmingham and Sheffield.

Mother of pearl panels were set in the lids, bases and sides of snuff-box frames. The lid panel might be slightly convex or flat and carved in three-dimensional relief with an all-over design. A typical pictorial scene might include figures such as dancers against a rural background surrounded by a border of flowers and foliage, itself encircled with a plain formal edging. The lid interior might be decorated with a picture in transparent paint which was illumined by the underlying radiance of the pearl, or set with a miniature portrait painted on ivory.

The peacock iridescence of mother of pearl snuff-boxes, displaying a colour range of reds, yellows, purples and browns, coppery greens and steely blues, is caused by the shell structure embodying microscopic furrows which run across the surface.

Snuff-boxes in every fashionable shape were assembled by goldsmiths who stocked sets of pearl panels and carved, engraved or painted them to the customer's commission and fitted them into silver-gilt mounts.

# CHAPTER 13

# Scottish Tartan Boxes

SCOTSMEN were prohibited by Act of Parliament from wearing their multi-coloured tartans between 1747 and 1782 when the ban was lifted. During this period tartans were considered by Englishmen to be badges of outlawry and Scotsmen wore grey shepherd's plaid. The wearing of clan-tartans was revived, however, at the time of George IV's visit to Scotland in 1822 and by 1828 clan-tartans were again fashionable. This gave James Sandy, a poor mechanic of Perthshire who had lost the use of his legs, the idea of making snuff-boxes of white wood with hinges also of wood. Each was decorated on the lid with a tartan design and the sides with sketches in indian ink protected by clear varnish. These snuff-boxes came to the notice of Charles Stiven, Laurencekirk, Kincardineshire, who pirated the idea and decorated snuff-boxes with sketches of huntsmen and hounds such as were fashionable on serving jugs in brown salt-glaze stoneware, recognisable views and rural scenes. Designs of meandering lines known as 'worming' followed and naturalistic subjects such as the fruiting vine. These were soon joined by designs in checks, at first in black, later in colours, a great variety of diapers being produced. From these developed the celebrated clan-tartan boxes in full colours.

The craft spread to Ayrshire and by 1832, according to *Chambers's Gazetteer of Scotland*, more than one hundred persons were employed in the clan-tartan woodwork factory of William & Andrew Smith at Mauchline, Ayrshire. This village was an obvious centre for souvenir work, being the home of many of Robert Burns's friends and of characters in his poems. The old kirk yard was the scene of his 'Holy Fair' and half a mile away was, 'that lovely cot Mossgoil'. Scotsmen at the time of William IV's coronation in 1831 carried colourful clan-tartan snuff-boxes enriched with gold or silver name plate. The Smith brothers' clan-tartan snuff-boxes and other articles, known contemporaneously as Laurencekirk boxes, were soon in such demand that a wholesale warehouse was established at 61 Charlotte Street, Birmingham.

The wood of the sycamore (*Acer pseudo-platanus*) was used exclusively because of its close even texture and light weight which gave the articles all the advantages of contemporaneous papier mâché. A length of rough wood costing 25s made snuff-boxes to the value of £3,000. This block was drilled with a series of circular depressions which were then squared out with chisels, filed and finished with glass paper.

Craftsmanship was notable for its excellence. The cover was attached by an integral hinge hand-carved and fitted partly to the box rim and partly to the lid with a precision equal to that found on some of the finest gold snuff-boxes. These well-fitting joints never worked loose and ensured a tight lid through which snuff could not permeate. The box and lid were lined with heavy tin-foil to prevent scent from the wood affecting the snuff. The ingenuity with which the large number of component parts of some snuff-boxes were assembled is remarkable. A small octagonal box, for instance, might consist of twenty-six different pieces, yet appear to be carved from a single block, so exactly were the parts fitted together.

The exterior surface was prepared for ornament by covering with ground colour. Until the mid-1840s a white ground was used for the tartans in lighter tones but it was found that black gave greater depth and brilliance to the overlaid water colours. Several coats of ground colour were applied, each rubbed with fine glass paper. The article was then ready to receive its decoration in imitation of a clan-tartan, about one hundred varieties being used, with Royal Stuart the most popular. An invaluable reference work for collectors is *The Clan-Tartans of Scotland* compiled and published by William & Andrew Smith.

A mechanical method of drawing tartans in colour was patented by William Smith of Mauchline in November 1853

(No. 2639). By fitting a single drawing pen into a simple hand-worked machine and using water colour it was possible to draw straight lines with ease and precision. The workman, with his pattern before him, could regulate the lines and spaces by means of a notched wheel. All lines in one colour were completed, the pen cleaned and the workman continued with a fresh colour. The patent specification states that Smith's snuff-boxes possessed three advantages over those designed by competitors: 'perfect securing when the box is closed; facility of fully opening and closing; exposure of the snuff to a greater or lesser degree as may be desired'.

The patent was superseded in August 1856 by a second patent (No. 1845) granted to Andrew & William Smith. In this, instead of ruling pens small wheels or rollers were used and for the first time oil and varnish colours could be introduced. This improved machine, operating several rollers simultaneously, was able to draw all the parallel lines of one colour at once. The patent specification noted that tartans could be drawn by this machine more cheaply than by former methods.

The colours used were selected to harmonise and the half-tints were created by laying on successive lines of pure colour, results being attractively rich in tone with a pleasing transparency. Although this method continued in use some less costly tartan patterns were printed by lithography from about 1860.

Snuff-boxes of fine quality might be ornamented more elaborately in this manner. Typically, the cover would carry a miniature painting in oils of a scene set against its appropriate tartan. A view of Scone Palace, for instance, might appear on a box decorated with the Murray tartan; Balmoral with the Royal Stuart tartan; Melrose Abbey with the Hunting Stuart tartan. The scenes were painted direct on the wood before the application of the tartan. They were restricted largely to Scottish views, particularly places celebrated in history and song, and to more generalised scenes of the chase and copies of Landseer's pictures rendered into colour from engravings.

After being titled and given its background tartan the article received two coats of clear varnish. This was smoothed with fine sandpaper and five more coats of varnish similarly treated. The article was then hand-polished to a highly glossy surface.

Men employed in this work were paid wages ranging between 16s and 24s for a 70-hour week, dependent upon their skill. Women earned 7s to 9s a week and children 2s. Artists skilled in copying in oil colours from black and white engravings were paid about 30s a week. Outworkers were employed also to carry out inexpensive diaper checkerings: these date from the mid-1840s and were catalogued as tartans. They were ruled on paper which was glued to small articles of wood. Circular table snuff-boxes, painted black, were decorated and varnished in imitation of papier mâché; their lids might be ornamented with tartans or with line engravings overpainted and varnished.

The Smiths labelled much of their finer clan-tartan work with their name and the words *warranted genuine*. Other makers' labels include those of Davidson, Wilson & Amphlet of Mauchline, who until 1841 displayed the royal arms of William IV (d. 1837) and the legend *Makers to His Majesty*. From 1841 the royal arms of Queen Victoria with the words *Makers to Her Majesty* appeared on the labels of Charles Stiven & Sons of Laurencekirk, often with the inscription *inventors and manufacturers*.

William & Andrew Smith also made snuff-boxes advertised from about 1850 as 'Scoto-Russian'. These imitated the costly enamelled boxes for long imported from Russia. The wood box and its cover were first covered with heavy tin foil. This was painted and when dry was placed on a ruling machine fitted with a sharply pointed scriber which traced an intricate pattern of curved and straight lines in imitation of engine-turning. These lines penetrated the paint but only scraped the tin-foil which was left shining bright, the effect resembling inlaid silver. Several coats of copal varnish, each polished down, completed the box. The Jury of the Great Exhibition, 1851, awarded the firm a gold medal for 'accuracy of workmanship, high degree of finish and beauty of varnish' in connection with Smith's 'Scoto-Russian' snuff-boxes. Their prices ranged between 22s and 168s per doz.

Clark & Davidson, also of Mauchline, from about 1835 issued a series of expensively finished tartan snuff-boxes painted with portraits of Prince Charles Edward inside the lids. These must not be confused with the valuable Jacobite propaganda snuff-boxes of the 1740s and later, which were in heavy wood but with hinged mounts of gilded brass.

# CHAPTER 14

# Miscellaneous

## AMBER

AMBER snuff-boxes were fashionable intermittently from the time of Queen Anne until the 1850s. The material had the great advantage of remaining warm and pleasant to handle in cold weather when a hardstone would chill the snuff and diminish its flavour. It was also conspicuously light to carry. The earliest reference so far noted is in Pope's *Rape of the Lock*. Boxes might be in solid amber but more usually frames of 18-carat gold were mounted with plaques of polished amber, the lid being slightly convex.

Amber, a substance traditionally regarded as a charm against witchcraft and magic, was long believed to be a semi-precious mineral, although Pliny described it as a resinous juice which had oozed from extinct coniferous trees and discharged into the sea. It is not of so great an age as hardstone: agate, for instance, is three times harder. Linnaeus confirmed Pliny's attribution in about 1750, declaring that amber was the fossilised resin of the prehistoric *Pinus succinifer* tree. This discovery brought about a decline in the use of amber in fashionable jewellery. The greater part of the amber used in the construction of snuff-boxes came from the Pomeranian coast of East Prussia, the king holding the monopoly and regulating the supply. Amber is of two kinds, marine and terrestrial. The former is thrown ashore during the autumnal storms and is either fished from the tideless Baltic with small nets or picked up by wading. Terrestrial amber was excavated in the form of small, crude fragments from alluvial deposits of sand and clay in mines sunk on the sea-shore.

Baltic amber is found in all shades of yellow, from the palest primrose and brown and red and often encloses the remains of small insects. In clarity it varies from a vitreous transparency to absolute opacity, some specimens suggesting ivory. This is rare and is used chiefly for carved appliqué work welded to a darker amber plaque for setting in a snuff-box lid. Amber from Sicily has a light reddish hue; Chinese and Burmese ambers are either yellow or red and usually cloudy.

Amber intended for snuff-box lids and bases was first split by a lead plate revolving in a lathe. The surfaces were then worked over with thin scraping tools, smoothed with a Swedish whetstone, polished with vegetable oil or chalk and water and finished by friction with a flannel held in the hand. During these processes the amber tended to become charged with electricity, very hot and even liable to fly into fragments. For this reason the pieces were worked in rotation to keep each cool and but feebly electrified. They were then ready for the jeweller to fit them into gold mounts. If the amber in a snuff-box breaks it may be repaired invisibly by smearing the edges with caustic potash and pressing them firmly together when made warm over a smokeless charcoal fire. The union is so perfect that no trace of the join is visible. Very few early Georgian amber snuff-boxes remain.

Terrestrial amber was of lesser quality, the fragments being fused into pressed blocks at the Dantzig finishing works. These blocks could be cut and worked into snuff-box lids. Snuff-boxes composed of amber throughout were cast in a piece and not carved as commonly believed. The process was outlined in *The Polygraphic Dictionary*, 1735: 'To melt Amber and cast it into any figure, with flies in it, as seen in those valuable pieces of Amber sold at a great price. Crush your amber and sprinkle it into hot turpentine, stirring it with a piece of fir wood until you find no resistance . . . keep stirring until the powder Amber is dissolv'd and thick enough to pour into moulds. When it is cold, you will have what figure you propose remain as hard as amber itself, with all the qualities of amber.'

Gold or silver snuff-box frames set with plates of amber were

9

fashionably carried in the daytime and might be circular, oval, rectangular, shell-shaped, or in basket form, the latter commonly of German manufacture. The amber lid was sometimes set with a gold-framed miniature. The sides of others were in gold skilfully chased in elaborate patterns.

As the century progressed gold and silver mounts became less elaborate and lighter in weight. Until 1798 the gold was always of 22-carat quality. Mounts in the early part of the 19th century might be cast in rather heavy metal and gold was of 18-carat quality. From 1854 gold of 15, 12 and 9 carats was used by the factory silversmiths; hand-worked mounts were in 18-carat gold. The majority of factory work incorporated plaques of pressed and polished amber from the Danzig workshops: these might contain insects of existing species. An amber snuff-box set in gold, made by C. W. Hoffman of Danzig, won for him a prize medal at the Great Exhibition, 1851.

Collectors must beware of imitation amber. This is made by melting together one part of pine resin, two parts of lacca in tabulis, and 15 parts of white colophony. This synthetic amber has none of the electrical power that lies latent in genuine amber.

### DAMASCENING

Damascening decorated some early and mid-Victorian snuff-boxes. The name was derived from Damascus, once celebrated for the quality of its intricate ornament on steel. This was a craft in which line designs or devices of gold or silver were sunk into black or oxidised steel, iron or copper. Fine line channels were undercut on the exterior surfaces and into these were hammered wires of contrasting colour until they were thoroughly incorporated with the metal of the snuff-box. The entire snuff-box was finished with a uniform level surface.

Very few gold snuff-boxes made in England were damascened. A well-known maker in gold and silver gilt fancy patterns during the 1860s and 1870s was the London goldsmith Barkentin. His work is always fully hall-marked.

ENGINE-TURNING

Decoration on snuff-boxes from the mid-1760s might include
intricate but wholly impersonal lines in geometrical patterns
mechanically incised. This appeared soon after William
Baddeley, Eastwood, Staffordshire, had established workshops
for the manufacture of engine-turning (known also as rose
engine-turning) lathes adapted for use by craftsmen of the
jewellery and fine stoneware pottery trades. The engine-turning
lathe had long been in use among wood turners, however, and
was fully described and illustrated in *L'Art de Tourner* by Charles
Plumier, 1701. This lathe rotated the objects to be decorated
with an eccentric oscillating movement, the cutting tool
remaining still. The machine could be so adjusted that the tool
would incise clear-cut shallow lines on any shaped surface in an
almost unlimited range of geometric patterns composed of
complicated chevrons, chequers, zig-zags, dice and so on. Lid,
base and sides of a snuff-box might be ornamented in this way,
each often displaying panels of different design.

NIELLO INLAY

A little-known series of silver boxes display inlay ornament.
Niello decoration was fashionable in England for about a
century from 1780 although fine Italian work dates to the 15th
century. This art consisted of cutting patterns with an engraver's
burin into the lid and sides of the snuff-box, such as scrolls and
associated designs. The deep incisions were filled with a black
semi-hard composition prepared by heating together oxides of
lead, copper and silver with sulphur. When cold this was
ground to a fine powder which was sprinkled upon the engraved
surface. A little borax was sprinkled over this and it was melted
over a charcoal fire, the mixture flowing into the lines cut into
the snuff-box. When cold the surface was smoothed and burnished, so that the niello produced the effect of a drawing in
black on gold or silver.

This process was not carried out in England until about 1840, a snuff-box lid often being worked with a presentation inscription. Some niello designs were engraved by Daniel Maclise, RA, with great delicacy, shadows being hatched with fine lines. In Georgian days the niello process was termed tulla-work after examples imported from the Russian town of Tulla.

### POTATO SKINS

Snuff-boxes composed of potato skins are recorded by George Evans in *An Old Snuff House*, 1921. Carried in the pocket, they could be relied upon to keep the snuff at its correct temperature for, as Mr Evans states, 'snuff is like claret – it needs the chill taken from it to bring out the bouquet. . . . These snuff-boxes were ornamented with a greenish lacquer, with a few fine threads of red or gold. The lids of some were hand-decorated with a crest, monogram or other means of identification.' The gilded hinges and fastener were, however, rather clumsy. Such boxes cost about twelve shillings each with little gold ornament. In the account books of Fribourg & Treyer they are entered as vegetable boxes. Mr Evans illustrates a rectangular example with bombé sides and a chased thumbpiece.

### BASSE-TAILLE

This decoration is only occasionally found on snuff-boxes. Colour designs were made by chiselling into the gold or silver and filling the incisions with coloured enamels brought flush to the surface and smoothed. Subjects were usually pictorial, including figure groups, landscapes, pastoral scenes and views of castles and great houses.

### WALKING STICK HANDLES

Long before the days of tobacco snuff a spherical pouncet box of gold or gilded silver containing perfume might decorate the head of a gentleman's walking staff. By the end of the 17th century walking sticks had become more slender and made of exotic woods. The cane-head remained a fashionable form of perfume carrier, usually spherical, occasionally urn-shaped. In Queen Anne's day it became a conceit among the exquisites to carry a pouncet-box or sponge-box in the snuff-pocket and use the cane head as a snuff-box. The hinged cover was opened by slight pressure upon a catch. Such boxes had become common by 1730. Doctors and apothecaries used them as receptacles for 'nutmeg or ginger to warm the stomach of the valetudinarian, or sugar candy for the asthmatic'.

Snuff-box heads on walking sticks were at first hand-raised from gold or silver-gilt plate and from about 1705 the lid of the spherical body might be secured by a simple bayonet fastener. Later some were of cast and chased prince's metal and from about 1730 of pinchbeck. The ivory crutch handle for a walking stick appears to date from about 1700 and from the early 1720s might be sliced horizontally and hinged, the interior excavated and fitted with a pair of utility snuff-boxes or with a snuff rasp.

# INDEX

*Illustration numbers are indicated in italic*